The Object
Technology
Revolution

The Object Technology Revolution

Michael Guttman
Jason Matthews

JOHN WILEY & SONS, INC.

New York • Chichester • Brisbane • Toronto • Singapore

Publisher: Katherine Schowalter
Editor: Robert Elliott
Managing Editor: Mark Hayden
Editorial Production & Design: SunCliff Graphic Productions
Text Illustrations: George J. McKeon

ISBN: 0-471-60679-0

Printed in the United States of America

10 9 8 7 6 5 4 3 2 1

Dedicated to our wives and families.
Thanks, Alisa, Michelle and the kids,
for your unfailing belief and support;
it makes all of our best work possible.

Contents

Preface

The title of this book indicates that it is about object technology, a worthy subject in its own right. However, this book is really just as much about change—a sweeping change that is sharply altering the way that all of us will look at business computing for some time to come.

Once it was enough for computing systems to just support the mainline, day-to-day operations of our business—general ledger, receivables, payables, payroll, scheduling, and so on. No more. Now we expect our business computing systems to do far more. Now they must provide information about virtually every facet of—and to every individual in—our increasingly far-flung, fast-changing enterprises.

In other words, the days when computing issues could be viewed as strictly operational and tactical are over. Instead we now need to squarely face the fact that business computing has become increasingly strategic—the very lifeblood of business decision-making. To put it bluntly, the ability to manage and leverage information is rapidly becoming the most critical delimiter between the winners and losers in an integrated global economy.

By now such thinking is hardly controversial, at least in theory. However, until recently, only a very few people realized just how profound this change in focus would be to their view of computing and computing technology. Many computer professionals simply assumed that the old style of computing—big machines running mammoth applications—would somehow be able to grow and adapt to meet these increasing demands for information.

We at Genesis realized more than a decade ago that something was fundamentally wrong with such thinking. We could see that large mainframes and monolithic applications could never take our clients to where they really wanted to go. Something new, we were sure, would have to replace the familiar behemoths of yester-computing.

Clearly, part of the answer included the PCs that first began proliferating everywhere nearly two decades ago. And another part of the answer included the increasingly flexible and inexpensive networks that tie together these PCs into configurations with more raw computing power than any mainframe.

But before these new computing platforms could really challenge the mainframe-centric view of the most computer users, we also felt that something else had to happen. We sensed that a whole new kind of software had to be developed that would take advantage of these platforms, and do so in a way that would change the whole way the industry thought about computing and computing applications.

Almost a decade ago we became pretty sure that this "brave new world" of computing would be built from a kind of software component called an *object*. At that time, software objects had been around for almost fifteen years, but were mostly the province of a few academics and advanced hackers. Except in a few areas like graphical user interfaces, hardly anyone had any idea how they could be applied to mainstream business computing problems.

Now, in less than a decade, all this has changed. Objects are rapidly becoming the "currency" of a new generation of systems and applications, and of an increasingly innovative way of thinking about computing in general. Everyone, it seems, is at least talking about objects and, perhaps even more surprisingly, an increasing number of mainstream business computing vendors—and users—are beginning to take objects and object technology quite seriously.

Computer book publishers are now just starting to address this growing interest in objects. Unfortunately, most of the rapidly growing list of available books primarily address technical issues, and largely ignore the general reader. So, while it is now easy to find books on object programming or object databases, it is nearly impossible to find a decent book on, for example, how objects are reshaping business computing, or why anyone should care.

More and more, we find that what most people really seem to want and need is a simple, straightforward, easy-to-read book describing objects, object technology, the industry standardization efforts and more from a business-oriented viewpoint. In particular, managers—both business and technical alike—need to understand clearly how any technology will benefit their enterprise today and help them plan a competitive strategy for the future.

At Genesis, most of our clients fit this profile. They really don't want to hear any more about *polymorphism, inheritance* and *void pointers*. Instead they want to know about where object technology is going, and how they can best take advantage of it; today and tomorrow.

These people are pretty savvy, whether or not they are strictly "technical." They already sense that business computing as we have come to know it is undergoing a radical transformation, and they already know something about how objects are a part of this. In fact, many of them have already come to many of the same conclusions that we discuss in this book.

But even the most savvy people still have a hard time explaining these ideas simply and succinctly to anyone else—for example, their boss! Moreover, it seems that no one else has as yet had the opportunity—or allotted sufficient time and energy—to write and publish a book about all these very important ideas, especially one that can be quickly read and easily understood by nontechnical and technical people alike.

That's where we came in. We were frankly sick and tired of telling our customers and prospects that we didn't know of a good book that would tell them and their colleagues what they needed to know about objects and the emerging object computing industry. Instead, we had to recommend books that, while full of interesting technical ideas, did not really paint the business picture these people needed to see about objects.

Fortunately, we were not the only people to realize that such a book was now absolutely necessary. We found out that the President of the Object Management Group (OMG), Chris Stone, felt the same way. In fact, it turned out that Chris had just such a book in mind when he first negotiated a deal with QED Publishing, now a division of John Wiley & Sons, to publish an ongoing series of books on object technology and its impact on the global business computing community.

This book, of course, is the result. Needless to say, we are honored to be encouraged by OMG to write this book and grateful for the opportunity of working with them on such a worthy project.

However, OMG and Genesis did not meet accidentally. Genesis has been an OMG member since shortly after its founding, and has for some years been on its Board of Directors, the only consulting company currently to do so.

Moreover, we've participated actively in many of OMG's technical activities, including its well-known Common Object Request Broker Architecture (CORBA), now the most widely accepted standard for distributed object computing. In addition, we also speak at its well-known Object World conferences, and have written for *First Class*, the OMG's newsletter.

We have been so active in OMG largely because we consider it the world's foremost popularizer of object technology. OMG has played a very critical role in the last few years getting the overall business computing community to begin seriously considering object technology and, frankly, this is very good for our business.

In fact, it is no exaggeration to say that, without OMG, serious business-oriented object technology might still be the province of a very few specialists and early adopters. Moreover, most of the computing public's view of objects would probably still be associated with little more than the cute icons they see every day on the video screens of their personal computers.

The results of OMG's vision and efforts are obvious even for a casual observer of the computing industry. A few short years ago, objects were practically unknown. Now, vendors are announcing object strategies, architectures, products, and alliances on a nearly daily basis. More importantly, object success stories from end-users, many for mission-critical projects, have become regular additions to the features sections of major computing publications.

All this, in turn, has accelerated and amplified the work of the OMG itself, as organization after organization has joined and taken an active role in its many ongoing activities. OMG has really grown up—some 400 members at this writing—and virtually every single major systems vendor is an active member. Names such as Sun, Novell, HP, Microsoft and IBM, just to name just a few, populate the OMG roster as well as dozens of smaller vendors, major systems integrators, and most importantly, end-users representing a broad spectrum of businesses from every corner of the globe.

The recent sharp increase of end-user organizations in OMG has been especially gratifying to us. OMG's earliest end-users tended to be the same classic "early adopters" seen in every advanced software forum. However, now we are regularly welcoming mainstream organizations that are making serious commitments to object technology. Even the most conservative end-users are nowadays watching object-related industry developments much more closely, and increasingly turning to OMG and its members for advice.

Yet, amazingly, this is the first book generally available that describe this *object revolution*, its impact on the computing industry, and role of OMG and other key players in it. Now we finally have something to give to the many people who ask us, time and time again, to explain why objects were important to them, and from a business perspective thank you very much.

Even before we began writing this book, these ceaseless questions forced us to constantly reconsider from the *outside in* every assumption we had gained building up our technical competence in objects from the *inside out.* These ideas always seemed worthy of a book, but, even so, writing that book wasn't easy. Explaining such ideas in person, it turns out, is quite different from distilling them all into something readable. We often struggled mightily to explain and illustrate ideas in writing that in person had always seemed to simply "roll off the tongue."

In any case, we hope that the results are truly worthy of your interest in this book. Once again, we would like to publicly and personally thank Christopher Stone, President of OMG, for his unique insight as well as his hard-driving enthusiasm for this project. We owe much to Chris and his peers at OMG and Object World and sincerely appreciate their backing in this endeavor.

We also want to thank the many other people who contributed directly or indirectly to this book. Our customers, most of all, contributed through their inquiries, questions, comments, and suggestions. We thank them all and encourage them to keep demanding better and better explanations as to why they should give a damn about objects (yes, you know who you are!).

Of course, we need to convey a special heartfelt of thanks to our family, friends, peers, and tolerant coworkers. Not only have they encouraged this book but in many cases have contributed to it through their comments and suggestions. For our families who have weathered the birth of this, our first book, we know that *thanks* can never adequately express our gratitude.

Finally, special thanks to you, the reader. Without your interest in object technology, there would have been nothing of note for us to write about! If you have any comments or suggestions about how we can better express the ideas in this book (or anything else that you want to tell us about directly), please don't hesitate to contact as indicated below. Once again, we really appreciate your interest, time, and attention.

Michael Guttman   Jason Matthews

mguttman@genesis.dev.com   jmatthew@genesis.dev.com

Genesis Development Corporation
10 N. Church Street, 4th Floor
West Chester, PA 19380 USA
Voice: (610) 429-1553
FAX: (610) 429-1554

The Object
Technology
Revolution

CHAPTER 1

Introduction

The premise of this book is simple. We are about to be engulfed by a massive revolution in business computing systems that rivals the introduction of the computer itself. The revolution has already begun in a few small areas of business. By the time it hits its stride, almost nothing about business or computing will ever be the same. Fortunes will be made by those who know enough to take advantage of the enormous business opportunities that this revolution is bringing—and lost by those who don't. Right now, no one completely understands why or how this revolution is taking place. Even those who see it happening around them seem unable to predict the impact it will have on the future of computing, let alone business in general.

This book is all about this growing revolution and how it will change the business world forever. There are also a few things this book is *not* about. It's *not* about computers because this revolution is not about computers, although a new generation of hardware is certainly part of the picture. It's also *not* really about the astounding growth of software, although that, too, plays a critical role. And this book is *not* about communications, although upcoming advances in this area are essential to the revolution's success. No, this book—and the revolution—is not about anything most of us have heard a great deal about. Instead, both book and revolution are all about—*objects*.

Now, if you've never heard much about objects before, you're probably wondering: "What the deuce are objects, anyway? And how could they be so important?" Or maybe you already know something about objects but have been under the impression that they're just another goofy computer fad, another heaping portion of geek-food for the pocket-protector set. You might even be thinking: Objects? A major business issue? Where does this guy get off? Of course, you might have already learned

1

a good bit about objects on your own. You might even have begun exploring some of the business issues involved. In that case, you're probably wondering: Why hasn't anyone written much about this before? I agree with you—it's really about time.

This book should answer most of the basic questions you have about objects and their long-term impact—and maybe a few detailed ones in the bargain. However, the book will be successful only if it generates twice as many questions as answers, because questions indicate that you understand the implications of objects well enough to appreciate just how important (and how neglected) this subject really is.

The important thing is to read this book with an open mind. Sometimes, I'll offer something interesting that seems to make lots of sense, but you'll wonder what the point is. Don't worry, the point generally follows soon after. Other times, you'll feel that I'm belaboring the obvious. Well, sometimes even the best of us overlook the obvious and appreciate an occasional reminder. I may even jump to conclusions that can't quite be supported by available evidence. My only defense is to remind you that this is, after all, an idea book, not a scientific thesis. Authors of idea books traditionally reserve the right to make some pretty brash assertions, just as you, the reader, reserve the right to brashly question any and all assertions made within these pages. Keep in mind, though, that the best ideas tend to be those whose validity can't be proven for a number of years. I'll also be questioning a number of key assumptions about business and about computing. Many people, maybe even you, have held these assumptions sacred for years. More than a few people have built their careers on these assumptions, and have a string of successes to show for it.

Well, times change. Maybe those assumptions were right on the money then, and all that success just proves it. But maybe all that success has taken us to a new plateau, a plateau where our old assumptions don't really work as well as they once did. And maybe, just maybe, we won't be able to climb much higher until we winnow through all those old assumptions and eliminate every speck of chaff that slows us down, even chaff that, until recently, held plump kernels of wheat.

Well, so much for the soapbox. It's time to take a quick look at what lies ahead.

WHAT LIES AHEAD

In the remainder of this chapter, I'll provide some useful background information on the computer industry in general. If you are already familiar with this information, feel free to skip it (or skip ahead to later chapters) as the spirit moves you. After all, this *is* your book.

Chapter 2 describes where the computer industry has been and where it is now. In it, I review the computer hardware and software revolutions that have set the stage for the upcoming object revolution. Later in the chapter, I hazard several guesses about where the industry might be heading over the next few years.

Chapter 3 could have been titled "Everything You Wanted to Know About Objects (But Were Afraid to Ask)." It tells you exactly what objects are, where they come from, how they are used, what they do, why they behave the way they do, and how they communicate. Not only that, but I even draw an extensive parallel between objects and big-city taxicabs so that the inner workings of objects won't seem so mysterious. After all, wouldn't you rather try to wrap your mind around the role of a Checker cab dispatcher than the role of an *Object Request Broker,* or the nature and purpose of a taximeter rather than the nature and purpose of *object state*? I thought so. Me, too.

Once you're securely belted into my object-taxi, you'll be ready for Chapter 4, which describes the subtleties of object relationships and object management, setting the stage for Chapter 5's discussion of the importance of object standards and a brief history of the Object Management Group (OMG) and other significant organizations that have been guiding the development and commercialization of object technologies.

Chapter 6 continues the discussion of object standards and the organizations that promote them.

In Chapter 7, I throw caution to the wind. I abandon the here-and-now and do a considerable amount of crystal-ball gazing, complete with well-founded cautions, courageous business-related predictions, and some astute (one hopes) technological revelations.

So, there you have it, all my objectives in a nutshell—except my most critical objective, which is to provide you with a significant return on the time you invest in this book. If you enjoy reading these chapters as much as I enjoyed writing them, I'm halfway to my objective. If you also begin to think and read and ask a lot of questions about objects, this book will have done its job in spades.

WHEN BIG WAS BEAUTIFUL

We sometimes need to be reminded that the opening salvos in the business computing revolution were touched off less than 50 years ago, and that they were fired from the unlikeliest of cannons—ponderous sheet-metal boxes crammed with vacuum tubes the general size and shape of seltzer bottles, banks of overheated capacitors, resistors, and other color-coded components baked in the heat of the glowing glass tubes, each bank woven into the electronic madhouse with enough heavy-gauge cable to electrify Montana.

These first monoliths of the information age were ridiculously expensive to build and even more expensive to operate and service. Their air-conditioning bills alone could bring tears to the eyes of the toughest corporate bean-counter. In fact, most people thought they'd never be much use to business. Yet, in a few short years, these computing behemoths provoked a revolution that not only affected how we process information, but also how we think about business itself.

The technology behind these new devices was fascinating, but the real attention grabber was their ability to help us manage our businesses more efficiently and to operate them on a scale difficult to imagine before the technology was conceived. As soon as they were introduced, those shiny new computers challenged every time-honored assumption we ever had about what businesses could do and how fast they could do it. For openers, computers drastically increased the amount of information that could be stored, processed, and reported. Computers also shortened the time required to make informed business decisions from that information.

The business of business—processing orders, taking inventory, collecting and dispersing money, and analyzing profitability—has never been the same. Once the large-scale computer made its debut on the business scene, dozens of exciting new business concepts were constructed on the firm foundation of tangible benefits cranked out by gargantuan mainframes. Only a few of the new concepts could have succeeded without the processing punch of those early, power-hungry monsters.

During the heyday of mainframe computing, the primary measures of system performance were raw speed and storage capacity. The bigger and faster the machine, the conventional wisdom went, the more information it could process and the more applications it could support. This pervasive argument for larger and larger mainframes came to be known as the *brute-force* argument by those who preferred more elegant solutions to the problems at hand. The brute-force argument held that ever-larger computers were the best way to manage ever-larger numbers of customers, accounts, parts, or what have you so that the business could grow and diversify at an ever-faster pace. Whenever the available capacity got used up, businesses simply upgraded their mainframe computers to the next faster, larger model.

This monolithic view of computing fit quite nicely with the optimistic business philosophy of the post-WWII period. Unbridled growth was the order of the day. Bigger and more powerful were always better, and the solution to every business problem was to expand faster and further to realize every possible economy of scale. The unvoiced business mantra on the tip of everyone's tongue seemed to be: The more customers, the more products. The more products, the more sales offices. The more sales offices, the more transactions. And the more transactions, the better the company leverages costs and the better the company controls its markets.

The real trick was to sustain growth without relinquishing one iota of centralized control. This tactic led to the growth of gigantic business bureaucracies in which each company provided the majority of its own support functions. These bureaucracies were highly proprietary organizations, loath to outsource or partner with anyone for fear of losing control over quality, price, customers, or intellectual property. Companies even managed their own hotels, internal air fleets, and limo services in their eagerness to maximize their centralized control over every conceivable aspect of their business.

The giant self-contained mainframe was the perfect tool to carry out business philosophies that stressed monolithic self-sufficiency above all else. The mainframe—with regular upgrades, of course—could be counted on to handle ever-expanding numbers of employees, customers, products, and transactions that a growing business generated. The mainframe and its ever-expanding team of support personnel could be counted on to provide ever-increasing computing capacity to the expanding number of functions required to support a growing business. At the same time, all the data and processing were centralized in a single, highly visible *white room* that could be lit up like a hospital operating theater and made many times more secure than the average Pentagon briefing room. What could be better?

What indeed.

THE NEW DAY COMING

The heyday of centralized, bigger-is-better business lasted more than four decades, and many among us are the wealthier for it in more ways than one. In the last ten years or so, though, the critical assumptions associated with centralized, ever-expanding business organizations have been under severe attack. These days, just about every Fortune 100 multinational seems to be enmeshed in a perpetual *downsizing* spiral (or, if you prefer a kinder, gentler euphemism: *rightsizing effort*) that requires the company to reassess its business goals and practices in hope of reducing bureaucracy while decentralizing corporate control.

Painful reassessment causes many corporations to jettison many inefficient and archaic ways of doing business. The traditional corporation, with its top-down control, monolithic structure, and layers of middle management, is a doddering dinosaur whose days seem to have come and gone. The nimble organization of the nineties reorganizes at will, partners creatively, and chucks the rule book out the window every time an unanticipated business opportunity appears on the horizon.

Meanwhile, on the technology side, these same businesses are also involved in efforts to streamline their business computing systems. And, once again, we are dazzled by the incredible capabilities of computer hardware—this time, in the form of a new generation of sleek microprocessors stuffed with staggering amounts of computing power in ever-shrinking packages. As one technowag recently observed, "If the same strides achieved by computer hardware designers during the past ten years had been achieved by America's top automotive designers, the average Chevy would now cost about $150, would go well over 500 mph, and would get better than 1,500 mpg." Not a bad buy, all things considered. Today, silicon goodies spew forth in unthinkable volumes from automated factories around the world. Far-flung Silicon Valleys (and Silicon Hills and Silicon Deserts) offer up tiny, crystallized miracles for a relative pittance in hundreds of new makes, models, and types of computing systems.

In the nineties, big is bad and laptop is beautiful. Previous measures of computing, such as processing speed and information capacity, are all taken for granted in the same way that low maintenance, good gas mileage, and 100,000-mile dependability are taken for granted by buyers of certain import automobiles. What the new technology really promises is a decentralized mode of computing in which a powerful workstation sits on every desk, loosely coupled to other workstations and specialized servers through high-speed, high-bandwidth networks. Ironically, these networks are themselves by-products of microprocessor technology—but that's another chapter in another book.

The idea behind this new technology happens to fit nicely with the emerging realities of an increasingly competitive global business environment. The new technology itself helps small and nimble businesses acquire basic computing capabilities at a fraction of their previous cost. A few PCs, a small network, two or three high-powered servers, and, *Shazam*, a small company has an entry-level, enterprise-wide computing system second to none—a system that can be expanded quickly and cheaply with incremental upgrades from a variety of sophisticated suppliers. These new realities change the economics of hardware and alter the very core of our perception of how business computing is done. In our brave, new decentralized world, a PC sits on every desktop linked via a server to a workgroup and, via an enterprise-wide network, to every other workgroup. We can retrieve any of the enterprise's information from any PC and display it in a form compatible with the business-decision process at hand. We can promptly communicate information on demand to all other interested decision makers inside and even outside the enterprise. A perfect marriage of new technology and new business realities is now well within our technological grasp.

THE HUNGRY LION

Like a hungry lion in a cage, however, we ignore the feast in front of us to focus on a juicy piece of meat just outside the bars. In our case, the meat just beyond our reach is a business computing environment in which the mainframe (or its superserver successor) still crunches through our daily transaction volume, but is no longer the primary focus of our computing world. Instead, a powerful network of workstations intelligently links a global business village of knowledge workers and decision makers, all sharing information and forming strategic partnerships at will, as business conditions dictate.

To snag that juicy piece of meat, we must create more than just a new generation of hardware. We also must have a new model of business computing and a new generation of software to support it. This new model of computing enables information and processing to flow freely throughout the enterprise from system to system, from application to application, and from user to user. It directly supports the movement of information among enterprises. The new goal is not raw speed and high volume, but ready access to timely business information presented in a useful format by any authorized user at any location and from within any relevant application.

Given this new reality, we might expect substantial changes in our thinking about how we analyze, design, implement, and deploy new systems. And, indeed, many new ideas have been floated for our consideration in recent years—structured design and analysis, integrated databases, client/server computing, distributed computing, artificial intelligence, parallel processing, and graphical user interfaces, just to name a few. All of these new approaches attempt to change how we build, configure, or present systems. The aim, of course, is quicker time to market, less downtime and maintenance, improved utility and usability of applications to business end users, and, most important, the ability of different but related systems to interoperate. However, even these new ideas have not curbed the computing industry's enthusiasm for creating huge applications that crank through a lot of data as quickly as possible.

Given a choice between buying a faster processor or embracing a new business computing paradigm, most computer professionals pick the new processor. They assume that an increase in speed alone always improves an application's utility, while a move to a new paradigm could well be costly and risky. Therefore, despite all the new technology available, a real change in our fundamental view of business computing systems has been slow to occur. Some of this reluctance to change is simple human nature. In many cities built before the dawn of the automobile, the width of major streets is still based on the turning radius of a team of horses drawing a common freight wagon. The space age still finds us measuring most of our everyday lives in such curiosities as feet, inches (the length of a human finger digit), and miles (a thousand paces of a fully equipped Roman legionnaire). And, in the nuclear age, we still honor our country with songs and stories about great battles fought with less firepower than you'd find in the average Los Angeles police station.

And so it also goes with business computing systems. Hardware gets faster, cheaper, and easier to install and integrate. The software that runs on the hardware just seems to get bigger, more cumbersome to design and implement, harder to install, and more tedious to maintain. Layer upon layer of operating systems, languages, tools, utilities, databases, and applications form the bars of the lion's cage that restrains us. The harder we reach out for that delicious piece of meat just beyond these bars, the farther away it seems to be.

THE EYESHADES HAVE IT

Not long ago, roomsful of clerks maintained the accounts of corporations by cranking out millions of transactions by hand. To reduce the eye-numbing glare of incandescent light, they wore the distinctive green eyeshades we now associate with such mind-numbing drudgery. Today, all of these clerks have indeed been replaced by computers, but their drudgery lives on in roomfuls of programmers cranking out millions of lines of application code. Those distinctive green eyeshades? They've been replaced by the antiglare filters on hundreds of thousands of computer monitors.

Today, we can make millions of transistors dance on the head of a pin, but we still produce computer applications by hand in the same way that day-to-day business transactions were recorded a generation ago. Study after study shows that most information systems organizations spend 80 percent of their time and effort maintaining existing systems, leaving precious little time to develop new systems. Productivity among American white-collar employees—the presumed beneficiaries of computer technology—has failed to improve for more than a decade. Has the growth of computer systems led to an absolute decline in productivity over the last generation? Of course not. Far from it. The number of programmers sitting in front of antiglare filters is still tiny compared to the number of green-eyeshaded clerks in the past.

However, we can no longer expect existing information technology (IT) departments—organizations that spend 80 percent of their time maintaining existing systems—to lead the charge toward a new break-through in business computing productivity. At least, not without a massive change in thinking. Sadly, the inescapable conclusion is that traditional information systems technology may well be an impediment to change, rather than a catalyst. If today's typical IT organization has indeed become a roadblock to business, what's to be done? To understand the fundamental nature of this problem better, let's look at the problem through the eyes of one of those unlucky souls who, before the advent of the computer, managed a phalanx of green-eyeshaded clerks.

The day our imaginary accounting department was first set up, it was a big boon to the business: It improved cash flow and the quality and quantity of timely business information, and it relieved some staff members of the tedious and error-prone task of running endless calculations. However, as the business grew, there were only two options available to our imaginary accounting manager: Increase the number of clerks, or make incremental improvements in the basic mechanics of the accounting process (such as streamlining the workflow, introducing desk calculators, ordering higher-grade mechanical pencils and less stressful desks and chairs, and, of course, buying a better grade of green eyeshades).

For the sake of argument, let's say that each improvement generates a modest increase in productivity. Some, such as introducing desk calcu-lators, might even be fairly significant. But, as time staggers on, every increase initially achieved will tend to flatten out. Eventually, no matter how good the tools of the trade become, productivity reaches an easily predictable upper limit: the number of transactions the average hard-working human can process by hand in a day.

As long as the company's business—let's say it manufactures suede shoes in various shades of blue—remains fairly stable, the productivity of the accounting staff presents no particular problems. But if the number of customers or transactions increases dramatically, the accounting sys-tem soon becomes a major business bottleneck. If, for example, it takes accounting three weeks to process an order, salespeople throughout the company will soon begin singing a sad refrain: "Hey, Hugh, you know those blue suede shoes? Three weeks, minimum!" even though dozens of pairs of blue suede shoes might be gathering dust in inventory at that very moment. In today's business climate, green-eyeshade businesses like these don't last long, no matter how big they've managed to grow in the past; so, eventually, our imaginary accounting manager will have a real problem. He or she must either increase accounting productivity substantially, or face the prospect of becoming the biggest contributor to a rapidly foundering business. The dilemma is unavoidable: No matter how cleverly productivity has been improved in the past, the manager simply can't continue producing the results needed for survival. A real breakthrough is called for here—like, oh, maybe a computer?

Sadly, nothing in our imaginary accounting manager's business experience has prepared him or her to discover that breakthrough, much less implement it and deal effectively with its consequences. With all those green-eyeshaded minions to manage, there was precious little time to think about breakthroughs, anyway. In short, if a computer fell out of the sky and hit the manager on the head, he or she probably wouldn't have time to notice. This scenario describes the exact dilemma most business computing organizations find themselves in today. The glory days—the era when anyone could look like a genius by computerizing some line-of-business processing activity that had an immediate impact on the bottom line—are over. To avoid acknowledging this uncomfortable reality, managers will try almost anything that promises to enhance the productivity of their development and maintenance staff: more and faster hardware, better code generators, improved software methodologies, new systems software, compilers, and CASE tools—you name it. Each of these solutions has been tried, and each has suffered the predictable drawback of diminishing incremental returns.

This harsh new reality seems all the more painful to us for two reasons: the first related to software, and the second related to hardware. On the software side of the IT equation, those glory days when IT could do no wrong were only a few, short yesterdays ago. How many of the brave IT professionals who led that first victorious charge into line-of-business computing are ready to admit that those great days are gone forever, or that the current generation of tools and techniques can no longer achieve the amazing gains of the recent past? Far easier to count the days to early retirement than to gear up for yet another gut-wrenching revolution in computing.

The second reason that this harsh, new reality seems painful to us has to do with all the good news on the hardware side of the equation. Hardware has been making some staggering price/performance gains for several years now, and seems positioned to accelerate those gains in the months and years ahead. Frankly, these remarkable gains create a highly embarrassing situation for business computing professionals. While software performance gains can and have been used to prop up sagging business systems, they also beg the $64,000 question—Why isn't their overall productivity keeping pace with that of hardware? Remember our old friend, the imaginary precomputer accounting manager? Well, a long procession of solicitous computer salespeople no doubt darkened the door until he or she retired, was fired, or finally bit the bullet and brought in a computer for a trial run. However, if he or she did decide to embrace computers, the decision was no ordinary, incremental one. Let's face it: Once a computer enters the picture, nothing is ever the same again.

ON THE VERGE

Let's say that our imaginary manager finally did embrace the wonderful world of computers. If so, the change would have been so radical that, within a few years, few if any green-eyeshaded clerks would still be processing accounting transactions in the company—or working for any of the surviving competitors, for that matter. True, some of those clerks might have been kept around—*sans* shades—to provide technical support for the computer. But the computer, not they, processes each transaction at many times the speed and accuracy of its human counterpart. You see how it works? A major computer revolution occurred because a few clever people took a few brave steps that departed significantly from any incremental approach under consideration.

Incredibly, we are now on the verge of a revolution in business computing more radical than the automation of transaction processing by the last generation of computers. This new revolution will automate most traditional forms of software development and systems maintenance, using the latest generation of hardware and a whole new generation of software tools. The vision of green-eyeshaded clerks cranking out accounting entries has been relegated to the history books. The spectacle of legions of programmers pounding out endless lines of code, each weary visage lit by the glow of an antiglare monitor, will soon pass into the annals of antiquity to sit alongside hair mousse, $100 sneakers, tofu cheesecake, and other obvious affronts to our basic common sense.

In the new business computing world, software applications will be built in much the same way that hardware is built today. Reusable modular components will replace custom-written code. Each software component will represent a single group of real-world business entities, such as customers, accounts, departments, products, employees, and so on. Applications will not only be easy to build and change, they will also require very little day-to-day maintenance and will automatically connect to all relevant components anywhere within or outside the enterprise.

This change cannot happen soon enough to suit most businesses. A major productivity breakthrough in business systems development and maintenance would remove major roadblocks to company growth and change, and would enable companies to adapt quickly to dynamic, new market conditions. Soon, programmers will be able to create, upgrade, and integrate supporting software within weeks, days, or perhaps even hours of a new business requirement. Only then will businesses remain competitive in our ever-accelerating, globally scoped economy.

Such demands are well beyond the capabilities of most IT organizations today. Of course, a demand for a ten- to one-hundredfold increase in transaction processing capability would seem completely unreasonable to our imaginary green-eyeshaded accounting manager. But just because most of us cannot yet imagine exactly how such improvements in software productivity will happen does not mean they won't happen. As a wise, old software guru observed the day IBM stock he'd paid ten bucks a share for a few years earlier soared to $126: "Well, I guess real life still has a lot more imagination than I do."

Make no mistake, the new revolution in business computing has already begun and will become the dominant force in business computing systems within the next decade. The real question is: What do we do about it? The revolution, though swift and certain, will not be easy or painless. Vendors must create a suitable new infrastructure of collaborating software and hardware, which must then be acquired, installed, and integrated by information systems organizations. During the same time period, a huge inventory of existing systems—each representing a massive investment of time, money, and experience—must be integrated with the new environment or migrated to it. A whole new generation of people must learn to use tools and techniques they've never seen before, and to cope with the host of practical problems that always accompanies pervasive change.

Will the promised revolution be worth all this trouble and expense? You betcha. If you don't believe me, just consider the alternative. Let's say the green-eyeshade types carry the day, and computing systems continue to limit rather than support major new commercial developments. Are you really looking forward to playing catch-up with all those international computer professionals who heeded the call early on and joined the revolution at its crest? I know I'm not.

The real problem for most businesses doesn't seem to be finding the wherewithal to support this revolutionary change, but finding the gumption to get started—or maybe just finding the gumption to learn *how* to get started.

BUDDY, CAN YOU SPARE A PARADIGM?

The first big step on the winding road to the business computing revolution is a tough one to take. Why? Because it begins with a very tricky question: What shape should this revolutionary form of business computing take? Someone somewhere must answer this question and begin building a consensus within the information technology industry. This answer, whatever it is, must find significant support within the overall business community as well. This first critical step is all the more difficult because it requires IT professionals and business people to embrace an unfamiliar paradigm, one that requires them to stop thinking about their problems in old, outmoded terms. Instead, they must begin to define, standardize, and promulgate a number of fundamentally new approaches to these tired old problems.

For reasons that I'll introduce in subsequent chapters, this new paradigm will probably revolve around an interesting business computing element called an *object*, because objects provide a unique basis for approaching and discussing business computing problems in a intuitive and effective way. But more about objects later; right now we're concerned with a far bigger picture. Whatever you may already know about object languages, object databases, or object methodologies, the *paradigm shift* we'll be exploring in these pages is far more fundamental than a simple change in tools or terminology. In fact, the shift to objects will require major changes in the way we think about and use business computing systems, not just how we develop the software for them. These changes will challenge most of our old assumptions about computing and many of our assumptions about business as well.

Make no mistake, the *object revolution* is already under way. Growing numbers of information technology vendors, business users, and consultants have already embraced it with a fervor usually reserved for favored relatives and freshly baked pastry. These revolutionaries are not just eager to get up to speed in a brand-new technology, they're excited about learning a significantly better way of viewing business computing problems in general. Through the Object Management Group (OMG), a rapidly growing worldwide industry consortium, these object computing leaders are creating a new and dynamic vision of tomorrow's business computing environments.

The real test of a revolution's staying power is recruitment. Any revolution that cannot attract a steady stream of serious, committed revolutionaries is doomed to failure. Speaking as one who has been gripped by the remarkable potential of objects, I encourage you to make the decisions necessary to drive this technology to the forefront of your own business computing planning. After all, the full potential of a worldwide revolution in business computing can't be realized unless the whole world shares the vision—that's why this book was written.

To give you fair warning, the next chapter begins with a short retrospective that explains how we have ended up where we have, and why we must continue to push ahead. Read it if you're interested; otherwise, feel free to skip ahead a bit, then come back later for your history lesson.

CHAPTER 2

You Can't Get There From Here

WHERE HAVE WE BEEN?

Nearly everyone has heard the story about the market study that IBM commissioned during the dawn of huge commercial computers. The study's purpose? To determine how many of those lumbering behemoths they could possibly sell. The study confidently concluded that 50 main-frames would be quite sufficient to meet the business computing needs of all major customers for many years to come, thank you very much. This study, always good for a laugh at Big Blue's expense, hints at a serious question that we might be wise to answer: How many of our own current assumptions are leading us down a similarly shortsighted path?

Like IBM's less-than-prescient market researchers, we often base our current assumptions on past experiences and realities. These experiences and realities are not infallible, but they're often the only ones we've got. Unfortunately, when things are not going as well as one might have hoped, past experience is of little value. We must return to square one and challenge each of our assumptions anew. This process, as we shall soon see, can lead to some unsettling conclusions.

Probably the most sacred assumption of business computing is that it's based on computing hardware. Now, don't get me wrong. It is still fashionable in many circles to give lip service to the importance of software and abstract notions, such as structured software engineering. But don't be fooled. Today, most decisions about business computing start with assumptions about hardware. How many people, given a tour of a business computing department, ask to see the overall business computing architecture plan? And how many ask how it fits into the

15

Fast Iron Is More Gripping than Foggy Abstractions.

corporation's overall business strategy? Very few. What everyone is really there to see is the big box with the whirring, clicking, blinking components. They want the lowdown on how many MIPs (or OLTPs, or Whetstones, or whatever) this little hummer can really crank!

A lot of this behavior is just simple human nature. Most of us would prefer to talk about concrete things, such as computers, rather than abstractions, such as software architecture plans. Clocking the speed of computer hardware is one heck of a lot more interesting than analyzing software. The former can be compared to test-driving a sports car; the latter to researching the theory of perspective in art—interesting perhaps, but hardly gripping.

A Hard and Fast Bias

In business computing, however, hardware bias (and particularly hardware speed) is not simply visceral; it also has a strong historical component. Let's face it: Until recently, the fundamental underlying business factor for nearly all decisions was how much hardware was needed, how fast it was, and what it cost.

For most of its short history, computer hardware was expensive, monolithic, proprietary, and, by today's standards, exceptionally slow. Today, however, dirt-cheap commodity chips with as much power as a ten-year-old mainframe are available all over the world. It's like getting more and more gallons out of smaller and smaller pots, then lowering the price of pots to boot! The press calls this state of affairs a technological miracle, overlooking the fact that it is a business marvel as well—one that just keeps getting more and more marvelous all the time. As each new chip generation emerges, it makes the last one look so underpowered and expensive that the economics of computing are drastically altered on the spot.

Soon this relentless drive to design and produce ever-more-powerful hardware in greater and greater quantities will eliminate the need to think about hardware at all. Hardware capacity will become a commodity so cheap, so powerful, and so modular that we will simply assume its existence the same way we assume the existence of air, water, electricity, or, perhaps more to the point, the telephone.

When the telephone system reached a certain level of saturation, it not only sped up existing business activity, it supported the opening of entirely new business markets and created opportunities that were simply uneconomical before. Our old assumptions about how difficult it was to communicate with remote markets were upended almost overnight, and business was never quite the same. Today, anytime you want to communicate an idea, acquire up-to-date information, or make a business deal, you pick up the telephone without giving its underlying technology a second thought. Similarly, as the cost of hardware becomes essentially irrelevant, we will be forced to question every assumption ever made about computing, not to mention business. For years, we have reached conclusions about the feasibility of business computing systems and the kinds of businesses that could be conducted economically, based exclusively on the assumption of limited, expensive hardware resources. We now find that we must rethink all of these conclusions.

Once Upon a Time...

Interestingly enough, in the very early days of computing, hardware was relatively small, modular, and inexpensive. An abundance of simple sorting, calculating, and printing machines, configured by switches or wiring bread-boards, found their way into organizations large and small. Accounting departments, marketing organizations, and engineering groups grabbed them up a bit like the PCs of today. In their limited way, these simple machines revolutionized the business environment of their day.

The introduction of the mainframe computer changed all that. The mainframe computer was first developed in the research labs of government agencies and universities, mainly for military use. Its sophisticated electronic switching could perform operations hundreds, even thousands of times faster than any previous equipment. These computers could execute bigger and more complex programs, and combine operations previously spread across several smaller machines into a single, streamlined process. At this exact point in computing history, bigger clearly was better.

There was a nasty catch involved in moving from manual systems or simple automated systems to mainframes: massive expense. The new technology was not only very expensive but also very complex. Individual vendors invested heavily to develop and support highly proprietary systems. They then had to sell their systems at astronomical markups just to survive. Only the biggest customers could afford such expensive systems, and even they could cost-justify the systems for only their most critical commercial and engineering applications. Organizations that bought computers used them for only one or two key applications—it was considered too risky to use newfangled technology for much more. But mainframes, and mainframe users, soon matured; the era of mainframe computing finally hit its stride.

Business began doling out excess mainframe time to lesser applications. The more applications a company ran on its mainframe, the larger the business base that the mainframe's cost could be amortized over. Lower costs led to more and more mainframe use and, ultimately, more demand for computing capacity. The easiest way to meet this need was for vendors to create ever-larger mainframes. It was considered easier to manage a single incrementally growing mainframe installation than several smaller independent systems.

Social and economic trends within the business community also favored the monolithic, centralized mainframe. Some social critics regarded large impersonal computers as potential toys for Big Brother, but Big Business was more than happy to use them as giant clearinghouses for corporate information. To this end, they employed armies of analysts to make sense out of all their data. The analysts might not know exactly what to make of every piece of corporate data, but their employers slept better at night knowing that all their business secrets were gathered together in one big, secure box.

For the most part, the equation was simple: As a company's operations grew in volume, size, and complexity, the size of the mainframe required to support those operations grew accordingly. Once a large corporation made the decision to embrace a given vendor, that vendor essentially became a highly paid order-taker for a long series of assured upgrades, expansions, and ongoing maintenance fees. When they weren't busy taking orders, vendors spent their time dreaming up new upgrades for which to take orders. Their success further encouraged users, who could now be assured that *their* vendor had been a good choice and would be around to hold their hand forever.

The Software Monolith

This warm and fuzzy feeling of stability encouraged users and some third parties to invest heavily in developing their own applications software. An explosion of custom software development followed the introduction of mainframes, creating a market for better software development tools. Developers began to move from tedious machine coding to higher-level business computing languages, such as COBOL, and began relying more and more on system utilities, such as *sorts* and *report writers*.

At the same time, the big mainframes began to sport more sophisticated *operating systems* (the software that controls the housekeeping operations of the computer). Improvements in the operating systems made writing programs easier. Over time, the operating system handled the management of more and more computing resources, such as disk drives, printers, and memory, insulating the programmer from changes in the hardware configuration. These new operating systems also allowed multiple programs or tasks to run simultaneously, with the operating system handling the switching from program to program automatically. This was called *multitasking* or *time-sharing*. Eventually, multitasking enabled each program to act as if it alone owned the entire computer, a clever device to ensure that two or more programs running at the same time would never interfere with one another.

This last improvement led to the notion of the *virtual machine*, a theoretical computing environment for each application that always appeared to be as big as it needed to be, no matter how much actual hardware was actually available at any given time. This allowed lots more and bigger applications to share the same computer at the same time. Of course, virtual machines run faster if they have more real hardware to run on. Therefore, the main effect of allowing lots more (and larger) applications to run was really to sell more hardware. As the real machine filled to capacity with *virtual* machines running applications, the solution was, of course, to buy more mainframe hardware to carry the load—a computer salesperson's dream.

However, one of the other results of this *virtual machine* view of software was that it tended to reinforce the notion that applications should be large and monolithic. Once the operating system gave each application its own, huge virtual machine, applications could keep on growing, essentially without limits. In simple terms, let's say that a new accounting application was expected to share the mainframe with a new inventory control application. In that case, each respective department probably saved considerable money on hardware—and hardware maintenance—over having two separate installations. Having achieved this large hardware savings, the company could now gain only a marginal advantage from any attempt to share in the costs of developing the software.

Of course, if an organization bought a software development tool, such as a COBOL compiler, or some additional systems software, such as a database, these costs were shared among the various application development groups. But, short of this, there was very little incentive to figure out ways of reducing software costs by leveraging it across many applications. In practice, this meant that even if the two applications duplicated lots of functions, they were treated separately because they were different applications. For example, they might both have similar (but somewhat customized) routines to calculate dates, compute customer balances, or manage account information.

In theory, these common routines could have been carefully isolated and the cost of their development shared among the two applications. But that seldom actually happened in practice, and then only for the simplest, most general routines. Because the real focus was on hardware and hardware costs, how could anybody really justify spending much energy trying to save on software costs? As we shall soon discuss, however, this general inability to significantly leverage software development and maintenance has now become one of our biggest business computing problems.

The Vendor Monolith

But back then, the idea of worrying about software independent of hardware was almost heretical. Until quite recently, the foremost checklist item when evaluating any software or software development tool was whether it would run on an organization's major computing platform. In other words, if your company ran on IBM mainframes, but the best computing system for one of your business areas ran on a VAX—well, too bad, but forget it.

Of course, the more decisions an organization made to develop or acquire business computing systems for its particular mainframe, the more investment it had in that platform and, therefore, the more incentive it had to continue to make such decisions. So compelling was this logic that it would lead to the powerful, worldwide dominance of a single vendor—IBM—in just a few years. In fact, so dominant was IBM that, in an earlier era, it might well have evolved to a regulated public utility!

As it was, IBM was not only able to stave off the government's famous antitrust suit, but also to maintain its dominant industry position. This was despite its conscious decision to allow various niche rivals, such as DEC, to grow and prosper. IBM could afford such generosity because these rivals were largely dependent on the same strategy as IBM itself—centralized computers with proprietary, monolithic software. Once IBM gained its preeminent position, no rival could possibly unseat it by using the same basic approach. The behemoths that IBM created during that period certainly had their virtues. Now, however, they have clearly reached their limits, and we are struggling to cope with a new, emerging business order. As a result, our view of computing has already started to change considerably. Let's now take a look at where we are today.

WHERE ARE WE NOW

In those halcyon days of IBM's worldwide computing hegemony, who would have predicted that Big Blue's eventual fall from grace would not be from a larger and more powerful machine, but from a tiny one—the PC? Even more ironic is the fact that IBM itself would help to make this wimpy processing unit a household name and manage to fund Big Blue's most successful future business rivals in the bargain.

Yet, in a few short years, the IBM PC and its simple Disk Operating System (ironically named after IBM's own mainframe DOS) would unravel not only IBM, but also most of its largest competitors. Today those pioneering computing giants who have managed to survive curse the luck of a new crop of companies—callow, young upstarts a decade ago—that now appear to rule the computing world. Even more telling, perhaps, is how many of the greatest of these new rivals produce little or no hardware at all, but prosper luxuriantly and solely from hardware's former stepchild—software.

To comprehend how radical the last decade of computing has been, you need only compare the typical computing environment of today with that of a decade ago. The mainframe is still around, of course, and continues to process the lion's share of operational transactions—payroll, accounting, inventory, order processing, and so on. However, beyond this facade of similarity, almost nothing is the same. First of all, there are the hundreds if not thousands of PCs and workstations (I'll use these two terms synonymously) settled into every nook and cranny of the business—churning out documents, cranking through spreadsheets, and running all manner of applications. Collectively, these workstations represent far more computing power and activity than the mainframe ever did, and their share of the total computing pie is growing rapidly. Many of these PCs have already been quietly performing these functions for more than a decade, and are becoming traditional in their own right.

More recently, observers note a rapidly increasing trend to tie workstations together into local area networks, and to further interconnect these local networks by some sort of enterprise-wide backbone network. Many of these backbone networks no longer depend on the mainframe at all, but merely gateway to it to allow access to data and legacy applications. Otherwise, these networks handle electronic mail and data sharing among PC users completely independently from preexisting systems, such as mainframes.

One big result of this new hardware infrastructure is that the mainframe is no longer assumed (or is likely) to be the primary platform of choice for new applications. The incremental purchase and maintenance cost of computing power on the mainframe is so high that no one really wants to add new demands that might require an upgrade. In a way, this is like power companies pushing for energy conservation because the cost of building and maintaining new generating plants is so high.

Moving Off the Mainframe

As a result, there are lots of new applications that simply don't make economic sense on a mainframe, but do on workstations. For example, a mainframe might be needed to handle processing for the millions of claims handled yearly by a large insurance company. However, using that same mainframe to track the movement of a few hundred pending cases through the legal department would be overkill, a task easily handled more economically by a single PC or small local area network.

Developing applications for workstations—and maintaining them—is also a lot cheaper and faster than developing traditional mainframe applications. Not only are the hardware platforms lots cheaper to acquire and maintain, but there is also an enormous amount of low-cost packaged software available on PCs and workstations, and much of it can readily be customized to support a wide array of end-user applications. New applications, therefore, are less likely to be developed on the mainframe and far more likely to be developed, if possible, on the PC using the macro languages of ubiquitous spreadsheets and word processors, new PC programming languages, or other modern development tools that run only on PCs. The more applications that are developed using such tools, the better they become, spurring on more applications, and so on. In short, the PC marketplace is caught in a feedback loop that will continuously lead to more, better, and cheaper software—and software development tools—for some time to come.

Besides decreasing costs and reducing time to market, building applications on a workstation has another big advantage—the power and bandwidth to integrate complex graphics into the human interface. This not only allows for intuitive interface devices, such as windows, buttons, and scrollbars, but also allows for the integration of multimedia formats—stored images, full-motion video, animation, sound, and so on, all with rapid response times. These new formats allow a whole new kind of application that is more powerful and easier to use than anything dreamed of before.

Putty for Power Users

Because of their many advantages, PCs and PC-based tools have become putty in the hands of the so-called *power users*. These are technically savvy users or analysts hired directly by user departments, who increasingly choose to write or customize their own applications rather than wait through a two-year IT backlog for a traditional programmer/analyst to become available. Frequently, these upstarts can create applications on the fly that run circles around the ponderous mainframe programs the IT department is still neck-deep trying to maintain.

Such empowerment is a major innovation from the business perspective. In the past, if we had a new business idea, we had to cost-justify it not only on its market merits, but also against the information processing costs it would likely generate. After all this effort, we might even be told that the project was impossible or unfeasible, given current computing technology or the priorities of the IT department—no matter what its business potential.

Finally, even if the idea somehow passed muster, we might have to wait months or years until the necessary computing systems were acquired or developed to support it. This might push the whole project outside of its intended market window. Clearly, only the most compelling projects could hope to get much more than a polite hearing in this environment.

Now we can often just buy a workstation and some database software, generate some screens on a visual editor, add some multimedia, and we're ready to go. Not only is this fast and easy, but it also may produce more usable and powerful software than anything possible on the mainframe. Even if we need access to data on the mainframe, there are interactive PC tools that make this easier and faster than writing traditional mainframe programs that do the same thing.

Now, the point of all this isn't to say that workstations are technically better than mainframes (they are just different, not better), but to describe how almost every assumption we have made in the past about business computing systems has been challenged by the new availability of cheap, modular hardware. This new hardware has created a whole new economic equation that allows computing power to be added anywhere in the enterprise at, from a business perspective, almost no cost.

All this has, of course, triggered a stampede to develop PC-based software at every level of the organization, and to install more and more

PCs and networks. In many organizations, new mainframe development has come to a screeching halt. Some of these companies are moving all new development to PCs, while others are even more aggressive. They actually want to port all their *existing* applications to PCs, networks, and superservers as well, and push the mainframe completely out the door.

The Mixed Blessing

However, much of this new PC-based software development is rapidly becoming a mixed blessing. Unless there is very careful planning, the catch to all this marvelous, new empowerment is that it can easily create a towering Babel of hardware, software, and data spread out across the enterprise, with little or no control or integration and lots of potential maintenance costs. Furthermore, just creating more and more applications, even improved ones, will increase business productivity only up to a point—unless they are highly interoperable. The term *interoperable* refers to the ability of different but complementary applications to access each other's information and functionality. Even if everyone is somehow physically connected to the same network, that's no guarantee that their application software and data can be shared or interoperate.

This interoperability problem has major implications for technologists—and for corporate business strategists as well. If applications can't easily interoperate, most of their value can't be leveraged by the enterprise as a whole, or by the enterprise's strategic business partners. And if applications can't be leveraged in this way, they will face diminishing returns over time—and eventually sink into oblivion under the weight of their own maintenance costs, just like our aging mainframe applications have.

The problem on both the PC and the mainframe is that each application tends to be treated as a world unto itself, running in its own *virtual machine*. Moving information from one application to another is a major chore, and sharing functionality is nearly impossible. For example, if we want to access a customer record maintained by our mainframe customer service system to do some market research on a new product idea, we have to hope that the data is some known form (e.g., normalized in a commercial database). Even then, we have to know something about the structure of the data, and replicate any computing functions already in the customer service program that may be handy for selecting or analyzing individual customers.

This essentially means writing a new miniapplication to access the data, and then inserting it into our market analysis software. Even assuming this can be done, it is likely to be expensive and time-consuming, and require the intervention of a skilled programmer/analyst with precise knowledge about the inner workings of the customer service system. And, of course, we'll be assuming the burden of maintenance if someone changes the customer service system. So, in effect, we have simply added to the future maintenance costs of that system. It may seem that we're having a harder time getting at the information than if it was in the hands of our worst competitor! As I mentioned, this kind of problem has already plagued business computing systems for years, and especially rears its ugly head when mergers, acquisitions, and strategic partnerships bring together existing systems that are not compatible. However, the problem is even worse as corporations create all of these new workstation-based applications strung across multiple platforms and networks.

In the mainframe world of old, we could at least expect all of our applications to use the same storage medium and filing system, execute in the same location, and use the same operating system and often the same programming language and database. While this certainly didn't guarantee full interoperability, it at least implied a certain minimum level of control and coordination in such areas as security, fault tolerance, and communications.

In today's polyglot systems environment, we have lost all hope of gaining such de facto control. At present, we are not even sure how to *locate* all of our applications and information, much less how to ensure that they all interoperate. The simple fact is that there are as yet no universally acknowledged techniques for creating applications for heterogeneous, networked systems that guarantee interoperability.

Of course, there are lots of formal industry standard efforts purporting to cover everything from presentation formats to filing systems to communications to query languages. Generating such standards seems to have become the classic way for vendors to claim that they really intend to support interoperability. The running joke is that standards are so popular that there are more and more of them every day! Unfortunately, this means that in the competitive computing marketplace, the much-vaunted idea of *open systems* has become a dream not unlike world peace—a noble but increasingly unattainable notion. Even today, customers are likely to take a new *open standard* seriously only if it is driven by a single, dominant vendor, making *open* something of an oxymoron.

The PC Monolith

The real problem is that we have taken the old mainframe notion of a monolithic application running in its own virtual machine and ported it almost directly to our new PCs and workstations. On mainframes, we had

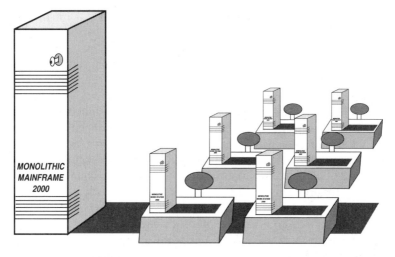

MONOLITHIC MAINFRAME VS. MONOLITHIC WORKSTATIONS

No Great Improvement.

a single machine running multiple monolithic applications concurrently. With PCs, we have multiple machines, each concurrently running a single monolithic application. And, as we keep going in this direction, we will soon progress to multiple superworkstations, each running multiple monolithic applications at the same time. This is hardly the direction in which we'd like to be heading.

It is no exaggeration to say that each one of these monolithic PC applications is, in fact, a business time bomb. Like its mainframe counterparts, each will require costly maintenance. And, as these various applications need to share information and processing, a separate gateway between each such sharing pair will have to be built. Furthermore, each gateway itself will be an application that will require its own maintenance if either of the gateway applications—or their shared data—needs to change.

Remember, the real problem we have here is not a hardware problem. Our ongoing advances in hardware and communications will, for the foreseeable future, always allow us to run more applications faster on more machines simultaneously. And, strictly speaking, it is not even really a software problem—although better software development techniques will certainly be part of the solution; that's what this book is all about. No, the real problem is a business problem, and it's worth stating out loud and displaying in a big box.

> How can we organize the business and its supporting technology to create business systems that leverage the information and processing in other systems and yet can respond quickly (and cost-effectively) to change? How can we get those systems to interact intelligently with each other and with all the users in the enterprise and its business partners?

We'd like to solve this business problem permanently so that our business systems will always be flexible and responsive to changing business needs. Before we start to discuss the solution to this problem, let's take a look at what is going to happen to the global business environment over the next few years that may have further impact on our thinking.

WHERE ARE WE GOING?

We all know that business is changing radically, transformed by intense global competition, rapid technological change, and ever-changing markets. We also know that the old idea of a rigidly structured corporation, with its many-layered chain of command, is a thing of the past—too expensive and too slow and top-heavy to change appropriately with the times. This continues to generate in many large corporations an almost continuous process of reorganizations, right-sizings, and shifting business alliances.

For most enterprises, such changes are wrenching and painful, spreading fear and panic through the workforce and frightening away stable investors and business partners. At the same time, however, a number of corporations are beginning to learn how to thrive on that kind of organization change, and to create management structures that work best in the kind of controlled chaos that still gives most of us the willies.

Increasingly, we are hearing about the notion of a *virtual corporation*, a possible successor to yesterday's monolithic, centralized establishment. Briefly, the virtual corporation is a business entity with a very flat hierarchy and well-focused skills set that makes its money through strategic alliances arranged among semiautonomous units of the corporation, or between those units and various outside businesses. Now, this is the second time I have used the word *virtual* in a definition (the first was the *virtual machine*). Is there some relationship? Well, none was really intended, but we certainly can see some superficial comparisons.

The virtual machine was designed to allow many different computing applications to simultaneously share the same hardware. The virtual corporation, on the other hand, allows many different partners to be coordinated at the same time to achieve the same task. Later on, I will discuss how these two *virtuals* will link up in a new business computing environment. For now, let's go back to looking at just the virtual corporation.

In a sense, some of the aspects of a virtual corporation already permeate the global business world. Few companies completely go it alone anymore or simply maintain rigidly fixed relationships with their suppliers and business partners. Such concepts as *outsourcing and comarketing* are well known and even fashionable. These are seen as clever ways to gain some leverage in areas outside of one's expertise without generating much overhead. However, many companies still enter into (or reassess) their business alliances only reluctantly. They usually consider partnering only when all attempts to handle their problems internally have been utterly exhausted. The process of managing such relationships is considered a necessary evil, an undercutting of the company's natural desire to directly control everything.

A true virtual corporation is specifically designed to maximize its business opportunities by partnering with others, and to generate and support new relationships at a speed that would be considered destabilizing in most businesses today. A real virtual corporation would *rather* find a partner than create a new department. It does not secretly want to own the world, but sure would like to be able to lease any part of it at a moment's notice! As a result, the virtual corporation has virtually no overhead. A small staff, often as few as five to ten people, can run an entire business that generates millions in revenue. This fact not only keeps overhead costs low, but also leads to quick decisions and an uncanny ability to respond to rapidly changing business conditions.

The Virtual Deal

In our ideal virtual corporation, we get an idea on Monday, set up a task team to study it on Tuesday, contact potential partners by Wednesday, and reach a decision (go/no go) by Friday. By the following Wednesday, we've set up financing, advertising, and marketing; we've consummated the necessary alliances and joint ventures; and, within a few more days, we're ready to start cranking out new business. Ridiculous? For certain lines of business today, such as setting up large-scale global financing deals, the competitive pressures are such that the preceding schedule might be considered rather languorous. But remember, with a virtual corporation, we are not talking just about radically reducing the time and effort to process a particular deal in an ongoing line of business, but sometimes that required to enter a whole new line of business!

Consider a company that handles the acquisition and installation of computer chip manufacturing equipment for such giants as Intel. When the customer identifies a need, a small staff can swing a deal among financiers, suppliers, and installers that can have the customer up and running as quickly as possible. Each deal is worth millions, and is a minienterprise in its own right. Not only that, but rapid changes in both the technology and economics of the computer chip industry require that this company retool its modus operandi with every deal. The real assets in a business like this are its strategic relationships with customers, financiers, suppliers, and service providers. Such a business carefully nurtures these alliances by keeping up with the latest developments in each. It also keeps shopping for new relationships that promise more business in the future.

If the Shoe Fits...

Okay, so we can imagine that some companies can make a great buck by keeping lean and brokering deals among others. But can the virtual corporation model work for more traditional businesses? And, of course, what does all this have to do with information systems, anyway?

Let's consider the question of a traditional business first. Suppose we own a shoe manufacturing company that has traditionally sold shoes (our only product) through distributors to retail stores. Now, suppose we're taking a bruising from imports in retail stores, so we decide to open a chain of outlet stores. At the same time, we begin to offer our shoes through a mail-order catalog. Now, for 100 years, we have thought of ourselves as a shoe company—the president even drives a car with the license plate SOLEMATE! However, we might now ask whether we are simply in the shoe business, or whether we are now also the retail outlet business or the mail-order business. If quarterly profits are down and pressure from investors or creditors is up, this may not be an academic question.

Having made the investment to get into these two new businesses, it is no longer clear whether our best option is to try to make and sell more shoes, or, for example, to expand the retail shops to include clothes and sporting goods. Of course, to do that, we will have to enter into relationships with other suppliers, locate new markets, change our advertising strategy, and so on. And to meet financial pressures, our makeover will have to be in high gear within a few months. In no time flat, our hidebound shoe company has become a candidate for a virtual corporation.

Strange as it may seem to some, an increasing amount of new business opportunities are now made or broken under time constraints measured in weeks and months, instead of in quarters or years. Businesses that cannot operate under these kinds of constraints will find their business base eroding, undercut by competitors who can. As this happens, large bureaucracies seem more useless and costly than ever, and companies will be forced to shed not only layers of management, but also marginal lines of business and internal services that can be more economically outsourced. This makes them more and more dependent on external relationships, and more and more like a virtual corporation.

The Software Pipe Dream

Okay, so now we know a bit about virtual corporations and how changing business conditions can force even the most staid, old-line company into becoming a lean, mean, strategic-partnering machine. But how about our second question—what does all this have to do with information technology? Well, there are several important points to make here. First, all of our discussion about the virtual corporation reinforces the idea that future value of information systems will not lie so much in processing and storing scads of operational information. The real value will be in making that information available to knowledge workers and business decision makers on demand in a variety of customizable formats.

To make the kind of decisions that drive a virtual corporation, information cannot be hidden within applications. It must be ready and available, in an intelligent form, and all the time across the enterprise. However, even if we could get the information now locked away in large, monolithic applications out into the open (let's say, with a brilliantly organized central database), our problems would just be starting. This is true because as soon as we have made our decision to enter a new business based on that information, we must quickly implement new applications and services to support that new business.

Of course, for these kinds of short-term opportunities, it would simply not be economical to build complete, new monolithic applications from scratch in the old way. Not only would this potentially cost more money than the new business opportunity is worth—it might also take longer than the life of the window of opportunity for that new business. So, at a minimum, we now need to create applications much faster than ever before, and for a fraction of the cost. These new applications must immediately be able to access and manage all the information already available from previous enterprise applications. And, by logical extension, these new applications must be prepared to readily share their information with any future applications; but just sharing information isn't enough. Since we can't afford to create new systems from scratch, we'll have to find a way to actually share the *processing* of all our information among our new, our existing, and our future systems.

If this already seems like a pipe dream, rest assured that it is still only part of our new requirements. That's because, as a virtual corporation, we need instant and constant access not only to our own information and processes, but also to those of our strategic partners. To put together the kinds of deals that the virtual corporation thrives on, all the various partners will have to be able to connect their various systems seamlessly so that that information and processing can flow unimpeded among them. This suggests that the core of our business computing systems will not be applications at all. Instead, we will have service-based components, each associated with a particular business process. These components, like our strategic partners, can rapidly be reconfigured to support new business opportunities. In other words, our information systems, like our business, would be composed of interoperable components that can be connected and reconfigured at will to meet a specific business purpose.

In our shoe example, for instance, our retail outlet store information systems would not be nearly as useful if they were tied exclusively to selling shoes, since they would then be difficult to adapt to selling clothes, sporting goods, or anything else. Even better would be if our retail system could hook directly into those of our new clothing suppliers so that orders were automatically generated when goods were sold. Better still would be if our supplier could analyze our sales data on his or her merchandise in real time at will to make better manufacturing decisions (or even ordering decisions with suppliers).

Clearly, this kind of flexibility is currently beyond the capabilities of even the most advanced IT organization. In fact, no single IT organization could ever make it happen by itself. Only the biggest organizations, such as a General Motors, can even hope to make a dent unilaterally, even in their main line of business. But let's put aside this rather obvious, if troubling, observation for the moment and try to imagine what business would be like if we could indeed construct the kind of flexible, component-based business computing systems that we have just described.

A Virtual Fable

It is eight A.M. and you have just sat down at your desk at Forever Footwear, sipping your first *caffé latte* of the morning. Forever, with just nine employees, was once a little shoe factory in your pleasant little Maine hamlet. Now Forever is a virtual corporation that controls 3 percent of the worldwide market for fashion shoes, hosiery, and legging accessories through its deals with eight major suppliers and four large retail chains. Forever sold off the last of its own stores five years ago. The old shoe factory is now a chic shopping mall full of other outlet stores where you shop from time to time. Overnight, the worldwide electronic meganet has already processed your electronic mail according to your personal specifications of the evening before. In the middle of the big screen above your desk is a picture of Martin, your counterpart at Just Leggin's, one of your major suppliers in Singapore, and your top priority today. The icon in the corner of your screen indicates that Martin is already in and specifically waiting for your arrival to discuss the proposition he sent off last night. With a wave of your hand, a preconfigured signal to your computer's visual recognition system, you are instantly connected to Martin; his video image begins to move and talk.

Martin is trying to close a deal to buy three more manufacturing plants in Brazil, but they currently make sports clothes and have substantial inventory he doesn't need. He called you because he knows you sell sports clothes and might want the inventory. Your possible purchase of the inventory is critical to his acquisition financing, which he must complete by this afternoon. Martin has regular access to your leggings management software and database, which he uses along with those of his other customers to project—and automatically process—orders. But Martin has no regular authorization to access your sports clothes information system, so he needs your help. With the help of your respective computer systems and the meganet, he hopes you can work out a deal by noon, his financing deadline.

You need to know how much the inventory is really worth to you, based on such information as pending orders, sales history, and so on. This figure must be matched against the actual inventory, currently controlled by an inventory management system on a computer in Brussels that leases capacity to the current owners of the Brazilian plants through the meganet. From these owners, Martin has the security authorization to connect to the Brussels system, an authorization he now passes on to you. Your system immediately links to the Brussels system, passing along the security key. The Brussels system connects you to the Brazilian inventory software and database, which your own sales and inventory systems query to figure out its current value to you. While you chat with Martin, your system computes a pricing structure and communicates it back to you. The pricing structure includes a number of variables to be resolved at the time of actual sale, including one based on available cash on hand.

Martin's no dummy, and he has already checked out similar leads with other customers and across the meganet global marketboard. Along with their quotations, your price offering is fed into his plant acquisition application, which he constructed on the fly over the weekend from bits and pieces of an applications library he bought from a software house specializing in acquisitions, plus Just Leggin's' own software library. The program suggests a confidence level for your bid being optimum at likely time of sale. The deal is set to close at noon, assuming certain conditions are met. But, by noon, market conditions have changed and the deal is no longer attractive to Forever because of changes in your cash flow position in Europe. Automatically, the system connects you to Martin, who is visiting the office of another customer at this time. No problem, however—Martin has full access to all his information at the customer's computer system, since the customer's system signed him in with a retinal scan when he entered the room.

On the basis of the new data, being updated graphically in real time on both your screen and Martin's screen at the same time, you and Martin finagle a bit. You both decide to include in the purchasing formula some price breaks for you on his company's leggings over the next three months; the value of those price breaks is gleaned from the interaction of his leggings information system with yours. Martin also brings some pressure to bear over the meganet on Just Leggin's' London banker to assist you in easing your European cash position until the transaction can be completed. The deal closes immediately, and the inventory is yours. Of course, your inventory, sales, and purchasing systems are updated automatically, and the goods are forwarded to the warehouse of one of your customers in Vancouver. As your sales system figured, the goods will arrive exactly in time to fill an expected order for that customer.

Your customer's own computing system in Toronto is, of course, informed of their upcoming arrival and a new lower-than-anticipated price. This lower price automatically generates a future retail price drop in his or her system. Tomorrow, several ads will appear prominently in specialty electronic newspapers distributed to selected consumers near major stores in Ontario. Those ads will announce a special sale price on certain sports clothes for the next two weeks.

Managing Change

Okay, so the stuff about the retinal scan and visual recognition system was a bit much, but what about the rest of it? Frankly, there was absolutely nothing far-fetched about the scenario on the hardware side, and certainly nothing terribly revolutionary on the communications side, either. This means that, technology-wise, everything I've just described could happen—if not right now, then easily within the next decade or two. If such a scenario were possible, it would not just be a revolution in computing—it would mean a revolution in business. For, except in a few limited areas, such as global finance, no one is able to respond to changes and opportunities at anywhere near the speed described.

Even in these areas, no one can construct computing systems to support whole new lines of business on the fly, then reuse those systems later in systems yet to come. That sort of capability, and only that sort of capability, would make the virtual corporation truly viable on a wide scale. So what's missing from this picture? Three things:

Missing Element	*Description*
Business Computing Model	An underlying model that accommodates the sharing of information and processing freely among diverse enterprises. Without this model, no amount of new computing power will enable us to leverage our business computing investments effectively.
Capable Software	The software must be capable of implementing the Business Computing Model. Unfortunately, none of the currently available crop of software or software development tools is even close to being able to do even the simplest things just described.
A Viable Plan to Manage Change	A viable plan to manage change in computing systems is the most important missing element. To be truly useful, our business computing systems must be able to adapt far more quickly to change than ever before.

Of these three elements, the third one, A Viable Plan to Manage Change, is by far the most important. Even if I could stop the clock for as long as I like and use the time to construct the perfect worldwide integrated software system using conventional techniques, it would continue to work only until the first change was required. Without a mechanism to manage that change, the whole system would fall apart one minute after the clock started again.

The Date from Hell

This point really struck home in a recent article whose author pointed out that the year 2000 is just a few years off, but that the date routines of many applications and several operating system components do not properly handle date arithmetic involving the next millennium. As a simple yet powerful example, he suggested just trying to enter the year 00 or 01 as part of the date setting function in the then-current version of MS-DOS—it simply doesn't work!

"My gosh! It's the end of civilization!"

The Date from Hell Reappears on Schedule.

The real problem is not that any *one* routine needs to be changed, but that thousands upon thousands of applications use date-related functions and most of them implement their own date-management routines. Even if only a few of them have this millennial problem, how can we be sure which ones? We'd need to examine every application just to make sure they don't blow up on January 1, 2000. Of course, what about January 1, 2001 or February 29, 2004—well, you get the picture!

If current business computing systems cannot manage even this relatively trivial (and, in this case, highly predictable) kind of global change, how can they possibly adjust in real time to changing market conditions, new government regulations, shifting business alliances, improved computing technologies, and so on. It is that inability to manage change, and to do so on a global scale, that makes the scenario we described seem like science fiction. Forget the retinal scan and visual recognition system—let's first make sure we all mean the same thing when we say *date*!

So, we can continue to improve MIPs and transfer rates and disk access times until almost infinity, and all this will help a little. And we can learn to manage data formats and present clever user interfaces—that will help a little more. However, until we do something really revolutionary about our software problem, all that will really get us is more diminishing returns. I call this the *business computing roadblock*, and, as it turns out, it's not really a *technical* problem at all.

Creating Software Is Closer to Sorcery than to Science.

THE BUSINESS COMPUTING ROADBLOCK

Everyone knows that hardware without appropriate software is useless. But try to explain software to most people outside of the computer community, and eyes will quickly glaze over. Hardware is no problem— just compare MIPs to engine torque, disk storage to warehouses, monitors to TVs, and networks to the telephone system. But what can you really compare to software? After years and years, software continues to exist in its own magical world that surpasses the understanding of all but an elite few. In fact, even among hardened computer professionals, software is often viewed as closer to sorcery than science. In this view, the developer starts with a set of tools (magic potions)—a compiler (eye of newt), an editor (tongue of dog), and a debugger (wing of bat). He or she then runs them together on a particular platform (the bubbling cauldron) and, by applying some cryptic techniques full of buzzwords (secret incantations), produces the desired application.

If this process remains a mystery to the end user, often so does the resulting application. To get the application to do his or her bidding, the user must usually apply further potions and incantations, which, if not delivered exactly as specified by the programmer, will lead to strange and usually unwanted results (a hex). Often this happens even when the potions and incantations are applied properly. Anyway, when such unwanted results occur, of course, only the programmer knows the necessary magic to lift the spell.

However, even if the sorcerer fails utterly, he or she can always claim that the desired result was not possible yet, but could be achieved with more newts, frogs, incantations, and, of course, more time and more sorcerers. This might be seriously frustrating to patrons, but without any viable alternative, the sorcerer remains a necessary, even esteemed, member of the community as long as he or she can deliver at least some goods that nobody else can.

How Now, Sacred Cow?

And so, for many years, the business community has maintained, even coddled, the information technology community at great trouble and expense just because programming the big machines was apparently the only way it could handle the ever-increasing volume of customers, products, and transactions that characterized most of the post-WWII business climate. No matter what gibberish was produced, the business accepted it as part of the necessary witchcraft to produce the required results.

Given the business climate, the idea that massive investments in ever-larger machines and ever-larger development staffs were necessary to achieve computing productivity was readily accepted. Frankly, it was not much different from the idea that ever-bigger steel plants or sales forces were always the right way to increase growth, market control, and profitability. And, if these massive investments failed to pay off, it only meant that further massive investments were probably required.

In fact, during all those years, very little happened to improve software productivity. Following the monolithic model of development supported so well by the mainframe, thousands of applications were created with huge benefits for business. But soon, the cost of maintaining these applications and the hardware to run them became the dominant activity of most IT departments. Huge backlogs developed and new development increasingly took a backseat to maintenance.

The 80 percent–20 percent Dilemma.

Over time, the business value of these original software development investments declined to a point where they were hardly worth the cost of maintaining. The huge price/performance gains that kept coming in hardware somewhat masked the underlying lack of improvement in software productivity, much as cheap fuel costs masked (as they still do today) the inefficiencies of our industrial system. Also, the introduction of the PC temporarily removed some of the pressure to produce new applications on the mainframe. As a result, businesses kept pouring more money into more or less traditional IT, even as they radically restructured other areas of the enterprise.

But, in the last few years, the business climate that fostered the ever-growing IT organization has changed dramatically. As companies everywhere restructure, spin off marginal units, outsource services, and enter into strategic alliances—in some cases, just to survive—there are no longer very many sacred cows. Traditional IT departments everywhere are under the gun to cut costs, reduce overhead, shelve expansion plans, and increase productivity. In other words, traditional IT organizations are now considered by many of their business colleagues to be part of the problem, not part of the solution. After years of disappointing performance, the company's IT unit is viewed as just another cost center, with little or nothing to contribute to the overall strategy or bottom line of the enterprise. The view of IT is so dim in some quarters that the notion of outsourcing the entire IT operation is a serious consideration.

At the same time, however, we know that new and better business computing software is needed more than ever to support the emerging business model—the lean, mean virtual corporation. Of course, the new software we are talking about won't look at all like traditional software, with its big monolithic applications, its expensive, cumbersome development process, and its huge maintenance budgets. This new software will have to be easy to build, easy to change, and readily interoperable with all other software. Without such a major software breakthrough, businesses will invest only incrementally in business computing systems, fearful of the long-term costs of maintaining new systems. But, without major new investments in such computing systems, the new business model cannot achieve critical mass, and global business stagnation is the likely result.

Now, certainly, a better model of business computing software is not the *only* requirement for implementing a new worldwide business model. Naturally, there are many other economic, political, social, and managerial problems to be solved as well, some of which are undoubtedly more knotty. However, none of this lessens the consequences of ignoring the current business computing roadblock. For, without a drastically new approach to business computing, the ability of businesses to interact, partner, and adapt to changing business realities will be severely limited. Intuitively, many business people already understand this and grudgingly realize that they will have to make substantial new investments in software technology in order to get the desired results. This is much like the conclusion that many manufacturing companies (at least, those that have survived) came to when they decided to bite the bullet and redesign and rebuild their obsolete, money-losing plants with modern equipment and techniques.

However, there is no way that these business professionals will continue to entrust that task to the traditional software sorcerers, or fund the endless acquisitions of the newts, toads, and frogs of the traditional software world. This would be tantamount to building a new auto factory with equipment and techniques from the 1930s. Right now, based on their previous experiences with IT, most business leaders are pretty gun-shy about spending money on major software development projects. They are more likely to hold the spending line on traditional IT and force business units to pay for their own IT on a project-by-project basis. But, while this is a reasonable short-term strategy, it will not yield the business computing breakthrough that is needed to move business into anything like the virtual corporation model—much like a new manufacturing strategy that requires some significant investment to build a flexible computing infrastructure to support the entire enterprise.

However, business people will still have to be persuaded to spend real money on enterprise-wide business computing again. They will not simply move from one software sorcerer to another. In other words, they need to be presented with a new model of business computing and software that they can understand and that appears to be directly synergistic with their new business goals.

So, to overcome the business computing roadblock, we all need a new way of thinking about software that goes beyond the monolithic model of the past. In the following chapters, I will discuss how this new thinking might occur, and how it will spur the creation of a whole new kind of business computing system. As these new systems come onboard, they will revolutionize not only how we all do business computing, but even how we do business.

Objects: Building Business Systems with Components

Chances are, you picked up this book because it had the words *object* and *business* in its title, but, up to this point, I've talked only about business. I haven't mentioned the O-word much at all, except to observe in Chapter 1 that objects are a lot like big-city taxicabs.

WHAT IS AN OBJECT, ANYHOW?

Don't give up on me yet, okay?—there's a definite method to my madness. And, speaking of *methods*, this looks like the ideal time for me to define the object-oriented term *method* and relate it to several other important object-oriented terms and concepts. Why wait until Chapter 3 to lapse into object-speak? I'll let you in on a little secret: Up until now, I've sidestepped detailed descriptions of objects and their inner workings because the subject is usually buried under a mountain of technical jargon written for programmers, database gurus, or software designers. Hand the average business person a book that weighs 20 pounds, costs more than three or four regular books combined, and reads like a science project run amok, and he or she will say, "Gee, I'll bet Pete over in the computer department would really get a kick out of this. How come you're handing it to *me*?"

On the other hand, if you *are* Pete over in the computer department (or one of his hacker buddies), you probably already know quite a bit about objects from a theoretical point of view. You hardly need to read another weighty, technical tome that drones on and on about objects and how they are surrounded by *methods*, how *they encapsulate state*, are arranged in *classes*, and on and on. Instead, I wanted to establish up front that when you're dealing with objects, you are not dealing with (yet another) convoluted technical subject; you're dealing with a strategic business issue, one with long-term global implications.

But, before I begin describing what an object is (and, perhaps equally important, why it's like a taxicab), I want to make clear that this subject is part of a very important set of larger issues. These larger issues, though complex, are worth studying because they will affect the ability of major enterprises and industries to reach their full business potential.

Frankly, if I thought it would dispel the notion that I planned to roll out a new whiz-bang computer language or a double-bad database, I'd deep-six the term *object* altogether; but it's too late. Not only is the term *object* out of the bag, it's already a growing business in the software world. If I didn't talk about objects, you'd probably wonder why such an important topic was ignored in a book about the future of business computing! And maybe you wouldn't have picked up this book in the first place.

Object, Behave Thyself

Okay, so much for my secret strategy; I'm ready to talk about objects. But what is an object, anyway? Ask the average computer-science dweeb and you'll get a lot of techno-jargon about classes, methods, encapsulation, polymorphism, and all the other spooky terminology of the art. Stuff that might be useful if you're looking to start a new software religion or you have a thing about programming languages whose titles contain lots of sexy little plus marks. The trouble is, none of this verbiage gets us to the real heart of what an object is, much less how an object might be used to further anyone's business goals.

In the last chapter, I talked about constructing computing systems out of reusable, self-contained components. Now we have a name for those components: *objects.* From a business perspective then, an object is often defined as follows.

> **Object:** a reusable, self-contained component of a business computing model.

There is nothing particularly exotic about objects. In fact, generally speaking, the more an object matches something we know and recognize from ordinary life, the more useful it is in the long run. You want a good example of a business object? I'll give you several for the same low price: In a sales system, such things as a *customer* or *account* or *salesperson* would

CUSTOMER

WAREHOUSE

INVOICE

ACCOUNT

ON SALE!

SALESPERSON

INVENTORY ITEM

Objects Represent Familiar, Real-World Things.

be reasonable objects. In an inventory system, objects might be such things as *inventory items* or *warehouses*. If you ran a computerized personnel system, you might work with objects representing *employees, departments,* and *pay grade.* "Wait a minute," I hear you thinking, "you mean to tell me that objects are just some kind of fancy records in a super-duper database?" Well, yes—but only if you restrict your view to the data portion of an object. A legitimate object is far more than just a bundle of related data stuffed into some kind of repository. Objects are also capable of *behavior,* and their behavior is what enables objects to act independently and in (seemingly) intelligent ways.

Each separate chunk of object behavior-code is stuffed, like the proverbial genie, into a bottle all its own. Each genie in a bottle is called a *method,* and a method's name is a powerful thing: Whisper it to an object and you trigger the behavior hiding in the named bottle. If you know the names of all the methods in an object, you are said to know the object's *interface.* Knowing an object's interface means that you know not only quite a bit about all possible behaviors of that particular object, but also quite a bit about all the other objects that contain the same methods, even if you know nothing else about them.

By convention, method names tend to be made up of two or more words squeezed together without any spaces between them—computers are easily confused by spaces—and the names generally provide a hint about the behavior that's hiding in the bottle. For example, what kind of behavior would you expect from a method named *DisplayCost*? Well, if the method happens to reside in a business-related object designed for U.S. markets, the object's behavior would probably be to display a dollars-and-cents cost figure on the computer screen. But guess what: A method with a British version of behavior-code hidden in its bottle behaves differently. When you whisper *exactly* the same method name, even though the method is residing in exactly the same business object in exactly the same application, the object will display a *pounds-and-pence* cost figure on the screen. Smart object, huh?

Are objects really smart enough to know which side of the Atlantic they live on? No, not really. Objects often *appear* to know their country of origin, the current interest rate on loans, and all sorts of other impressive stuff, but only because some software wizard somewhere figured out a clever way to stuff shiny, new, country-specific (or any other *-specific*) behavior-code into every method in a given program *without* rewriting a single line of the program's code. *How* they do it isn't important right now; the fact that they *can* do it is—and that fact has serious implications worthy of your attention.

Okay, you have a rough idea of what objects are and how their behavior is controlled. A software engineer would probably want to point out that each time a new chunk of behavior-code is stuffed into a named method-bottle, the *specific implementation* of the behavior is changed but the *interface* (the method name) that *invokes* that behavior remains the same. Think of the possibilities: A few handfuls of data and a few well-chosen collections of methods can be combined into dozens of different collections of objects that, if carefully designed, can change their *specific behavior* in response to changing business conditions without requiring any significant changes in the software environment that creates and supports the objects.

What other important kinds of behavior are objects capable of? Well, all objects can send and receive *requests* via some form of centralized dispatcher-object, and they can implement those requests because they know enough about the interfaces of all their fellow objects that they can trigger the required behavior—and that is precisely why objects are like big-city taxicabs.

Thought I'd never get back to the taxi analogy, did you? Well, stick with me through this next bit of imagineering, because we're almost ready to pull into the taxi stand—and that's where you'll find the final key to understanding objects in all their confusing splendor.

What is meant by behavior? When you're talking taxicabs and other real-world entities, the term *behavior* can be defined as follows.

Behavior: the various things that real-world entities are capable of doing.

Behavior is considered *predictable* if it varies only when the stimulus varies. Ring a bell and Pavlov's dog salivates. However, if you ring a bell and the mutt sings four bars of "Home on the Range," his behavior isn't exactly what most of us would consider predictable. For example, if you were to call a New York cab company to request an airport run for yourself and six other business associates, you'd know exactly what cablike behavior to expect:

1. The dispatcher will ask you to provide some expected information as part of your request, including your current location, your destination, a pickup time, and the number of people in your party.

2. The dispatcher will decide which of the many *taxi*-objects that are currently up and running is the exact taxi-object for you—in this case, it's a seven-passenger, limo-class taxi that makes airport runs from your general neighborhood.

3. The dispatcher will pass your *request* (and all that time-place information you provided) to the appropriate limo-class taxi.

4. The limo-class taxi, behaving in a predictable, taxi-object manner, will arrive at the appointed place at the appointed time and whisk you to your destination.

The limo-class taxi, like all good taxi-objects, keeps several pieces of related information hidden (*encapsulated*) behind that thick Plexiglas wall you push the money through. Some of this information, such as the trip log and cash box, is considered private. Only the driver can alter or report this information. A reasonable arrangement? Sure. If each passenger could get at the cash box and trip log, these important pieces of information might get so fouled up that they would never accurately reflect the exact state of the taxi-object during every moment of its daily operation.

Other information inside the taxi-object, such as the driver's name, picture, and hack number, is mounted in a frame on the Plexiglas wall and changes every shift. This information is considered public—it's available for inspection by any passenger-object (or policeman-object) who requests it.

All of an object's public and private information taken together is called *state* because, like a snapshot or a surprise audit, it reveals the exact *state* of an object at any given moment in time. Encapsulated state information is *variable*—it changes value from time to time. Drivers change cabs, cabs change locations, and traffic conditions can force cabs to change routes and even rates. Because state information can vary so much over time, each kind of variable state information is given a descriptive name—trip log, route sheet, taximeter, cash box, hack license, and so on. This way, a cab driver knows exactly how to find and report the value of each piece of state information encapsulated in the average big-city taxi-object, even if he or she is from Sri Lanka and is driving the taxi through the heart of downtown Los Angeles.

Now, even though state information changes all the time, the requests made by big-city passenger-objects are the same the world over. What's more, passenger-objects know that their requests will trigger the same sort of taxi-object behavior the world over. Stand on a curb in downtown Hong Kong (or Houston or Hamburg) and wave your hand up and down. Zap! A herd of taxi-objects will appear at the curb directly in front of you—unless its raining or after 10:00 P.M. Climb in and say, "Fourth and Broadway," or the local equivalent in a commanding voice, and, once again (assuming you and your cabbie share a common language and there *is* a Fourth and Broadway in the city), the taxi-object behaves in a predictable manner.

Remember back a few pages when I defined an object's interface as the set of methods the object contains? I lied a little. Actually, an object's interface is made up of all of the methods *plus* a description of the specific information associated with each method. A *request* usually contains three things: an ID number that identifies the object that is the recipient of the request, a method from the object's interface, and an exact value for each piece of required information. Our taxi-object's interface, for example, contains a method for each type of behavior you've come to expect from a big-city taxi. The taxi-object uses the information that you furnished as part of your phone request to alter or update the *state* information that it keeps safely encapsulated behind its Plexiglas wall. (Remember, the trip log, the cash box, and so on?) Each request travels from a passenger-object or another taxi-object to an intermediary that I'll call a taxi-dispatcher-object (in object-oriented circles, it's called an *Object Request Broker* or *ORB*, but I'll tell you all about ORBs in a later chapter). The dispatcher-object locates the appropriate recipient and forwards the request. Assuming that the request matches one of the request-information patterns specified in the taxi-object's interface, the taxi-object *implements* the request by reacting with some sort of anticipated behavior.

Most objects, including our limo-class taxi-object, are collected into helpful groupings and subgroupings based on significant similarities in their behavior and state information. These groupings, called *classes* and *subclasses* for reasons that I'll go into later on, can help objects anticipate the basic behavior to expect from each other.

Object class (or subclass): a helpful grouping of objects based on shared behavior and other significant similarities.

Limo-class taxis, for example, might be described in object terms as *objects of the limo subclass, which is derived from the taxi class.* The limo subclass represent a helpful subdivision of the taxi class because the behavior and state information of limos is different enough from other kinds of taxis that the dispatcher treats them in a completely different manner. True, they share some behaviors with all other taxis (in object-oriented words, their subclass is *derived* from the taxi class), but they also have some behavior and state information that is unique to their own subclass—slower acceleration, softer handling, different methods of billing for services, and so on. The truth is that you can divvy up groups of objects in just about any reasonable way that makes sense. You decide that want to add a new object subclass to make things easier or less confusing, say, a new taxi subclass called the *limo-with-bar* subclass? Go ahead and add it in—no big deal. Object classes are designed to be flexible.

Okay, now that you have been introduced to the innards of taxi-objects, it's high time to transfer these basic object concepts to a more businesslike class of objects: *item*-objects. Since I'm making up these *item*-objects on the spot just to demonstrate how objects work in general, let's say that the unique behavior and state information that makes these *item*-objects alike—that makes them a unique *class* of objects—is that each *item*-object not only knows (*encapsulates*) its own price, but also holds the *methods* (behavior implementations) that can change that price, or even calculate its own cost based on a predetermined costing algorithm, such as FIFO or LIFO. This predictable set of *item*-object behaviors enables us to combine several item-objects into another object called an *automated inventory*-object.

Ready to let your imagination out another notch or two? Good. Picture an item-object that is designed to spit out a list of all the other item-objects from which it is assembled. This behavior would enable a

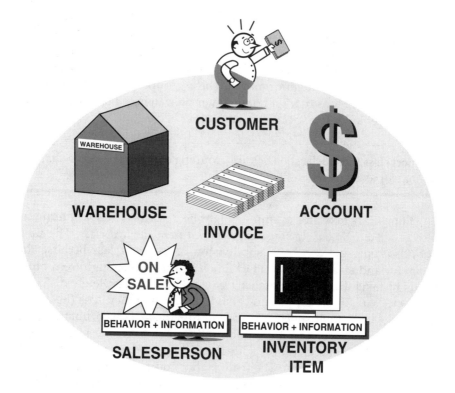

Objects Hold Behavior As Well As Information.

hammer-item-object to spit out a three-item list containing a *head*-item-object, a *handle*-item-object, and a *wedge*-item object to keep the head-item-object from flying off and shattering a *window*-object. Not a bad trick for a bunch of software abstractions.

The point is that an object like our *item*-object is not just the *data* (state information) that is encapsulated in it, but also all the different kinds of behaviors implemented by the object that enable other objects to manipulate the object's encapsulated information or any other information associated with the object. The behavior associated with these operations is at least as important as the information within the object or the structure in which the encapsulated information is stored.

Of course, we've always had behavior associated with information in our business computing systems, but, until we started to think about objects, we never had a very good way of expressing the *combination* of information and behavior. Instead, we've traditionally buried the implementation logic for executing that behavior deep inside our large, mono-

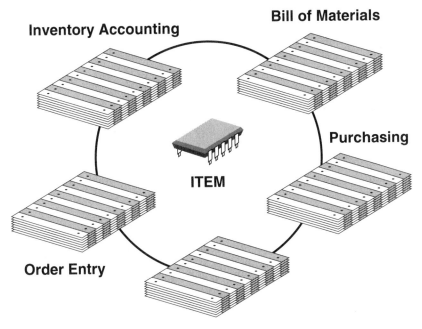

In Many Systems, Applications Have Their Own Cost Calculations.

lithic computing applications, separate from the information to which it relates. In short, the behavior resides in a labyrinth of code, while the information or data sits in files or databases.

Given a certain piece of information, there has been no particular way in traditional systems to determine all the behavior associated with that information. Given a particular piece of behavior, there has never been any particular way to figure out all the data or information it might operate upon. For example, let's say you want to know the computed cost of that *hammer-item* we invented earlier. In this case, the hammer-item represents a real hammer that you can inventory and sell. In a traditional system, you first would have to figure out where the information associated with that item lived. Then you would have to figure out where all the item-costing logic resided within our suite of inventory-related applications. You can see that you're facing a huge amount of work to figure out how to achieve a simple, straightforward result.

In a traditional system, no single computing entity contains a description of both the information and the behavior of a business entity, such as an *item*. Each new program must laboriously reconstruct that relationship for itself. Suppose that more than one application has to know, for example, how much a given *item* costs. In that case, the entire logic for inventory-costing must be available to each of these applications. It also has to be updated in every relevant application whenever any of the relevant rules change. What a nightmare!

A Business Issue

Now, at this point, you might be asking, "Well, this certainly sounds like a pain, but isn't it really just a problem for the computer department?" If you think about this problem a little more closely, you'll see that it is not just a computing issue, but a serious business issue as well. That's because, to stay in business, we all must constantly adapt to external changes in business conditions and initiate new activities. This means modifying our own business rules and consistently applying the latest ones to those new activities. But, to effectively apply or change these rules, we must know every location where the current rules are being followed and what business entities are affected. More and more, this includes the computer systems used to support your business. If, for example, the government changes the way you can compute inventory cost, you have to know every location in your current inventory computing system where such calculations take place. The same is true if you decide to offer a new line of business that requires access to your existing inventory items.

As savvy businessmen and businesswomen, our goal must be to make sure that such changes will affect a minimum of areas within our business computing systems, and that those areas are well defined and easily to locate. If not, we will soon be overwhelmed by the ever-increasing number of changes that typify the modern business environment. A simple analogy should suffice: Suppose that the telephone company produced telephone handsets that required detailed knowledge of the current telephone switching network in order to operate. We know that the implementation details of the telephone network are certainly likely to change, and change often, to incorporate new technology. But, in our analogy, every time the telephone company upgraded its telephone network, every telephone would have to be reconfigured to deal with the changes in that network service.

Of course, this is a ridiculous scenario. If true, it would prevent any incremental improvements in telephone service from ever occurring. The cost to retrofit all those telephones every time a network upgrade occurred, plus the costs generated by the disruptions in service each upgrade would cause, would be far too prohibitive. As a result, very few network changes would be economically feasible. Only really big changes with enormous payoffs could even hope to be justified—and they would involve tremendous costs and risks.

Fortunately, the real telephone system operates on a much more rational basis. What we really have today is a *class* of *telephone*-objects talking to a *class* of *telephone-network*-objects. From a *network* point of view, each telephone-object is simply an object that sends it a valid set of tones or pulses. From a *telephone* point of view, a telephone-network-object is an object that receives those tones or pulses and has all the necessary behaviors to create a connection to another telephone-object.

In this *object-oriented* telephone system, we can make any incremental change to either the network-object or the telephone-object, as long as they both continue to communicate with the same set of tones and pulses. We can substantially upgrade the network with fiber cable or a new electronic switching system, and no telephone-objects would have to change. At the same time, we can introduce new classes of telephone-objects—fax-objects, cellular-objects, and computer modem-objects—that don't look at all like the original telephone-object, all without directly affecting the network. All of these changes can occur incrementally, and none is really very risky.

Telephones or taxicabs, the concept of encapsulating information in objects that share many predictable kinds of behavior is always the same. In object terms, the object *interface* (the request list that triggers behaviors) that exists between the telephone class and the telephone-network class remains the same, even though their *implementation* (the specific details of the behavior) may change substantially. This separation of the interface of objects from their precise implementation is so important that I introduced it earlier and am revisiting it now so that you'll have two opportunities to grasp the importance of separating an implementation (the exact chunk of behavior-code that resides in a method and carries out an object's predictable behavior) from its interface (the method-name-information combination that invokes the method capable of achieving that predicable behavior).

Let's get back to our earlier *item* example. I imagined up a class of objects called *items* that, when requested, computed their own cost and automatically spit it out so that we could see it. Whenever you want to know the cost of an item, you just ask the item itself because all the appropriate rules about inventory costing are either encapsulated in each *item*-object or available to it. Anybody can make such a request anytime from any application.

But wait, it gets even better. Let's say that you decide to change the business rules for computing inventory costs of items from LIFO to FIFO, or some other formula altogether. In the new, improved object-oriented system, all the rules about item inventory costs are contained in one place

Inventory Accounting

Bill of Materials

Purchasing

ITEM

Order Entry

Commision Tracking

Item-Objects Know How to Calculate Their Own Cost.

for all item-objects—technically known as objects of the item class—not replicated in each application. You have to change the rules only *in one place*—the place where the *item* class is described—and the cost-computing *method* (the specific way in which cost-computing is implemented) will automatically change for all relevant applications.

Fortunately, in most business systems (and in normal, everyday life), the *way* we make requests for things changes relatively slowly, even if the way in which we *implement* those requests changes radically and often. When you pick up the telephone to make a call, the actual mechanism that connects you to the other party may be totally different from 20 years ago, but the way you make the request to be connected has hardly changed at all. Ditto with requesting a taxicab ride to a big-city airport or asking an inventory item-object to calculate its cost.

So, when you develop your business computing systems with objects, you solve a very important business problem. With objects, you can respond rapidly to incremental changes in your external business environment. As your business rules change, only a few of your object classes are likely to be affected—the rest of your systems can go on as before. And, as you add new systems, all the rules associated with the objects they use will be followed, because none of the rules is external to the objects themselves.

A Breath of Fresh Air

The whole point of this discussion of objects, requests, and interfaces is really quite simple. If you could describe all of your business systems as objects, the definition of major object classes in the system would be remarkably stable, as would their interfaces to one another. You could then change your implementations of these object classes at will, without forcing changes in the applications and other objects that use them. This fact alone represents an enormous change in current thinking about business systems, and particularly about business computing systems. In the past, when designing such systems, we have generally worried up front about hardware platforms, operating environments, languages, and databases—in other words, implementation issues. This is because any problems with, or changes in, the implementation of monolithic applications could bring down the whole house of cards.

By comparison, objects are a breath of fresh air. When you look at computing systems as a set of business-oriented objects, you can create business computing systems whose implementations are easy to change and upgrade, often for years to come. Such changes can be easily accommodated at the technical level (new platforms or software environments) and at the business level (changes in business rules and procedures). The trick is, of course, to keep the interfaces stable, even as you change implementations at will.

Amazingly, various versions of this object-oriented approach have been applied for years to manufacturing, communications, finance, and even computer hardware, *but seldom to business computing systems and software.* Our emphasis in the past was *to get things done*, not to adapt to change. As a result, it never really occurred to us to find a viable technique for creating truly reusable, self-contained business computing components—until now.

Objects really provide a way to design business systems, and the software that supports them, as a set of modular components. The basic technique is as old as Henry Ford's Model T and has proven effective in a variety of other industries over the past few decades. Unfortunately, our current business computing roadblock consists of four things we cannot continue to ignore:

- Glacial development times
- High maintenance costs

- User-unfriendly systems
- Resistance to change

Until we correct our deficiencies in these areas, we cannot create the tools that business requires to move confidently into the next set of global economic opportunities. So, as I observed earlier, objects are not primarily a programming, database, or even a design issue, but a very significant *business issue*. To really understand the business impact of objects, recognize first that business computing systems must be built from reusable objects with well-defined interfaces. Then recognize that it is up to all of us to bring about this important revolution in the confused world of business computing.

DO YOU TAKE REQUESTS?

In the previous section, I discussed the fact that every object class has certain predictable behavior, and that this behavior can be invoked in any particular object by making a request. For example, you can request an inventory *item* to calculate its cost. I also stated that the form required for making that request is specified in a well-defined interface for each available object class.

Now, the basic notion of a *request* seems like a simple one—you use it all the time in everyday life and take it pretty much for granted. However, your ability to make requests of others, to have those requests reliably delivered through intermediaries, and to have confidence that those requests will be properly fulfilled and acknowledged are pivotal in many areas of life, including business computing. These very same abilities will be necessary for success in business computing systems in the future.

If you doubt how important it is to be able to properly make a request, just spend a few days in a foreign country where nobody speaks your language and you don't speak theirs. You quickly find out that you if don't know the proper way to make a request, you can easily use up most of your time and energy just trying to obtain the necessities of life. And you'll likely experience quite a bit of hunger, thirst, and other forms of discomfort in the bargain. Which is why one of the very first things every baby learns in life is how to make appropriate requests. There are really two parts to every request: the general form of communication—typically the native language that everyone around you uses to format and deliver requests—and the specifics of the exact request.

Object-based systems work on a very similar set of principles. Within a given system, all of the objects must speak the same basic request language. In other words, there must be the same basic mechanisms for making and receiving requests for all objects, whether they are big or small, simple or complex. In most object systems, a request is also called a *message*, and I will use these two terms synonymously from now on.

Like humans, one of the very first behaviors that objects acquire is the capability to communicate requests or messages. No matter what other features it has, every object-oriented scheme contains a mechanism for delivering messages among objects. Earlier I said that the interface of an object class specified the exact form of the requests or messages that could be sent to an object of that class; it's the same in real life. When you take money out of your bank account, you request that *bank*-object give you so many *money*-objects in such and such denominations. Typically, you'll also have to provide some sort of information, such as an *identification*-object—your bank card or your driver's license, perhaps. If, on the other hand, you march into your bank-object without this information and shout, "I want all your money, and I want it now!" you might be issuing a request, and the request might even be recognized as part of the bank-object's interface, but the behavior it triggers might be a little more robust than you bargained for.

The interface for a given object class contains the entire collection of all possible requests that can be made to any object of that class. The complete interface is like a menu of all the services that each class of objects can provide, as well as a road map showing exactly how to request them. By looking at the interface you can answer two all-important questions:

- Does this class of object have the services you're looking for?
- Do you have all the information necessary to make the request you want to make?

At the Heart of the Matter

In any case, having an orderly system for making requests, and for determining which class of objects can service which requests, is at the heart of every object system. It's also at the heart of every business system. The idea in both cases is to break down the requirements of the system into a set of collaborating entities, or objects, similar to the notion of a company with departments. These departments coordinate by sending each other messages with requests for action or information.

The messaging mechanism allows the different departments to utilize each other's services without becoming too intertwined. As a result, for example, the accounting department can manage itself independently—change its internal procedures, hire and fire its own staff, buy new equipment, move to Mars—even though it is constantly processing requests from many other departments. As long as the accounting department can continue to process accounting-related requests as specified in its interface, it's doing the job specified in its charter. Meanwhile, the other departments don't know (and don't care) anything about the internal operations of the accounting department or how they change. These *user* departments simply need to know how to make valid requests for accounting services.

Similarly, let's consider what happens when the accounting department itself requests some services from another department. Let's say that accounting needs more supplies, or more office space, or simply wants the heat cranked up on a particularly cold day. When a need like this arises, accounting sends a message to another department, just as messages are sent to it. To send a message, accounting must know which department supplies the service and exactly how to request it. But, once again, it does not have to know anything about how any of these other departments actually *implements* its requests. As long as the accounting department fills out the required pencil requisitions properly, accounting does not really need to know where the purchasing department obtains pencils.

Object systems work exactly the same way. When you design an object-based computing system, you typically begin by identifying what the major objects are going to be. Then you define the interfaces of each class of objects based on the likely service needs of the other objects. You can design each object more or less independently, allowing each to send messages to all the other objects through their interfaces. Over time, the internal details of implementation within these objects is likely to change often, but the interfaces the various objects show to each other will change at a much slower pace.

A Real *Kool* Story

Why is this kind of division of labor and messaging mechanism so important, among both business systems and object systems? In manufacturing, such specialization was first introduced largely as a way for each department to become vastly more efficient at what it was doing. For example, let's say I work in the painting and finishing department of Kool-It! Inc., an air-conditioning company. Now, if all I do is paint air conditioners, I can get very adept with a paint machine, painting many units per hour and making few painting mistakes. I probably couldn't reach this level of productivity if I handled three different air-conditioner production tasks, spending only one-third of my time on painting.

Increased productivity is a very good reason for creating departments, but there is actually another more compelling reason for doing so:

to isolate and manage change. Let's go back to your paint department. We all know that, over time, the specific tasks involved in painting are likely to change as paint technology changes, the paint market changes, and government regulations about painting also change. If a single department wasn't responsible for painting, everybody in the plant who had to paint something would have to keep up with all the changes in all these various details of the painting industry. Of course, this would be true not only for painting, but also for hundreds of other jobs in the plant. Without specialization, one of two things would happen: either everyone would spend every available hour in training, or there would be no practical way to incorporate changes into the plant's day-to-day operations.

Prudent specialization, however, limits the problems associated with each change to a single, well-defined organizational area with a known set of interfaces. Most operational changes can be accommodated within a single department without affecting its interfaces to other departments. This object-oriented encapsulation strategy makes it possible to effectively manage that change. A separate paint department allows painting technology to change radically without affecting any of the other departments of the Kool-It! plant. The other departments might wonder how the painting department is managing to crank out three times as many units in half the time for 80 percent of its previous budget, but their curiosity won't affect how they made a request to have something painted. Therefore, it won't really affect how those other departments are operating.

The notion of specialization is so powerful in business that it normally goes on even below the department level. For example, within the Kool-It! paint department, one worker just worries about regulations, while someone else worries about technology. This division of responsibility means that only a few people are affected by any particular change.

Managing Change—Again

Given the rapid pace of change in most businesses today, operating without some kind of departmental structure that has a set of known, stable interfaces would be disastrous. Any company that tried to keep all of its workers apprised of every technology, market uptick, and procedural change would soon flounder in a morass of detail. Therefore, you can see that the most important reason for organizations to specialize, departmentalize, and implement a clear request/interface mechanism among departments is to isolate change. Once it is isolated, change can be managed effectively without disrupting basic operations.

The same point can be made about business computing systems. In traditional systems, we may have a conceptual business entity called a *customer* that is used in many systems. However, each system has its own way of interacting with a customer, an interaction that is buried deep within its own implementation. There is no single place where you can go to interact with a given customer, and no clearly defined, published interface that tells you how to access a customer. As market conditions, government regulations, and technologies change over time, you may be compelled to change many of the details of how you manage a *customer* and his or her related information. You must hunt and peck around in every system, hoping to find every place that might be affected by a particular change. This hunt-and-peck process increases the cost of change, not to mention your natural resistance to it.

Remember the Date from Hell that I described earlier? The year 2000, when many existing computerized date routines will no longer work? Remember that I described how we'll all have to drop everything to root around in every system to find and fix the problem? Well, imagine the advantage you'd have if you'd already implemented all of your current business computing systems with objects. If you had, each system would know that *date* was an object class and each *date*-object had the same interface that triggered a few different internal implementations in response to a request for the current date. To fix the Date from Hell, all you would have to do is find the bogus internal implementations hidden inside a few objects and fix them. Worst case: If you found that you needed to change the *date* interface, you would have to locate every other type of object that ever sends a message to a date-object and update the date interface in each one—a little more work, granted, but still no big deal. Mentally multiply this problem with dates across all the other business entities you deal with in your business computing systems and you'll begin to understand how traditional business computing systems obstruct change (albeit unwittingly), and how an object-oriented, message-based system would facilitate change in a significant way.

Pundits may claim that object systems are faster to write or that they yield programs that are inherently more user-friendly, can be debugged faster, support newer platforms, and so on. All this may be true and wonderful and of tremendous *technological* interest, but none of these reasons is compelling from a *business* viewpoint. As long as business people view objects as yet another technology to write better software, objects will, at best, make only incremental inroads in all but the most technology-driven companies.

However, the fact that object technology can help business computing systems react more quickly to ongoing change is a fact worthy of serious consideration at the highest levels of the enterprise. In fact, as the next section indicates, object-oriented, message-based systems can respond better to change than can their traditional rivals. Object-oriented systems also help business initiate and incorporate change. And, in the final analysis, it will be a company's ability to initiate and assimilate rapid change—not just respond to it—that will spell business success in the near future.

How will the potential of object-oriented approaches to business computing systems be realized on a global scale? Read on.

OBJECTS, OBJECTS EVERYWHERE

As I pointed out earlier, the real problem in business today is that to survive and prosper, the enterprise must not only respond quickly to change, but must also be able to create new opportunities by initiating change. This solution means a constant stream of new products, new services, and new business relationships introduced at much greater speed and in much greater volume than ever before. In this atmosphere, the traditional business enterprise model—where new ideas come from flexible startup companies that are unencumbered by the bureaucracies of older, larger companies—is increasingly unworkable. If these object-oriented ideas are big winners, startup companies could become big companies in their own right. Startups that don't do so will be vulnerable to acquisition by one of the older, larger traditional companies. In either case, the larger enterprise will probably provide the stability, capital, and infrastructure necessary to grow the business to its maturity.

This basic model is still around, but it is under increasing pressure. Global competition and technological change are accelerating mightily. The market window for new products, services, and marketing strategies is getting smaller and smaller every day. Instead of counting on a few very large opportunities, organizations must aggressively and constantly pursue a greater number of smaller opportunities, each with a shorter life span and an increasingly limited return. To seize these opportunities, large and small organizations must enter into strategic relationships much more quickly and easily. Any organization with a bright idea must be able to quickly assimilate and leverage the skill sets, manufacturing capacity, financial strength, and marketing clout of a variety of potential partners to have a significant chance of turning that idea into revenue while the window of opportunity is open. To move slowly is to risk losing the opportunity, not just to the competition, but also to that rapidly closing market window.

For example, consider Green Globe, Inc., a (mythical) small environmental research and development organization with a bright new product idea for converting urban garbage into playground toys, such as jungle gyms and swing sets. Ten years ago, the market window for such an idea might be five to ten years, easily long enough to grow the company to a size attractive enough to lure acquisition or venture partners, after which the product can be brought into the mainstream market.

Today, however, the rate of economic, technological, and regulatory change may dictate that the market window for such a product might be only two or three years. If Green Globe can't produce a working prototype that will convince several cities to embrace its products within the next 18 months, currently available funds may be committed to other, more competitive waste-recycling efforts. If this happens, Green Globe may not get another crack at its target market for four or five years. Of course, 18 months is not nearly long enough to grow up within a traditional business development model.

To get its idea to market, Green Globe may decide not to grow at all. Instead, it may partner with one or more other firms to get the financial, manufacturing, or marketing help it needs. For example, it may lease manufacturing capacity from one company, use the marketing channels of another, and finance operations from a third. By leveraging off the existing infrastructure of others, it can potentially put together the necessary elements to bring its idea to market several times faster than with a traditional business development model.

The Urge to Partner

The urge to partner has become a dominant characteristic of modern business. Even among long-standing competitors, constant announcements of strategic partnerships, joint ventures, comarketing arrangements, joint standards efforts, and so on are standard operating procedures. I expect this trend to continue and accelerate. Of course, this *urge to merge* is limited by the effective cost of putting together the partnerships. We can really consider only opportunities for which the cost of entering into the necessary relationships does not exceed the potential benefit to any one party.

One very important limiting factor to forming such relationships is the cost of information flow among the various partners. To make an informed decision to partner, each partner-to-be must have access to considerable information about all of the other parties, information that is typically locked up somewhere in those partners' business computing systems. Any inability of each party to directly access the other's computing systems means that partnering decisions must be made from fragmented and incomplete information. This substantially increases the risk of such ventures to all parties. Even more important, once a partnership is consummated, the partners must regularly exchange operational data and, in many cases, tie together portions of their individual computing systems. For example, Green Globe must be able to effectively coordinate the production of its manufacturing partner with the demands of its marketing and sales partners, and to project its requirements from the financial partners. To do these things, Green Globe must have regular access to the information systems of all three partners. This kind of business systems integration is called *interenterprise* computing, probably because it rolls so trippingly from the tongue.

Very few organizations seem to be able to get at their own information effectively, let alone engage in on-demand, *interenterprise* computing. Let's assume for the moment that we are dealing with a company whose systems, though traditional, are brilliantly organized and have served them well internally. Although Green Globe's information systems are relatively well structured and well understood internally, it is still impractical to imagine that outside organizations will be able to master Green Globe's systems quickly enough to use them directly. There is also the problem of isolating the information and processes that reasonably should be made known to any of Green Globe's partners from other information that should remain private.

In the traditional computing systems model, the only way we could possibly achieve these goals is to create a custom application to handle the partnership's operations. However, building yet another complex, custom application is something we'd really like to avoid at all costs. First of all, it could be very time-consuming and costly to build (further limiting how small an opportunity was worth exploiting). But the really disturbing prospect is that the new application would have to be maintained during the life of the venture. The 80-percent-maintenance-20-percent-development nightmare rises up to bedevil us all over again. That maintenance would require coordinating the new system with any changes that occur in any of the partners' relevant systems. In Green Globe's case, this might limit the changes GG would be able to make in its own internal systems—hardly a perfect situation. The thought of this nightmarish burden alone could be enough to put the kibosh on even the most lucrative of prospective partnerships. What IT director of sound mind would agree to head up such a project?

Objects to the Rescue

What does all this have to do with objects? By this time, you may have guessed that the gloomy picture I've just painted brightens considerably if we can assume that all partners have object-based business computing systems. As we shall discuss, the problem of integrating different object-based systems is not totally trivial. However, it is a darned sight easier than anything that might be attempted with traditional systems. Furthermore, as the object industry matures, it is likely to get easier still.

You might be thinking at this point—"Boy, this guy is really out there! Does he really expect me to believe that, just because business computing systems are developed with objects, they will be able to talk to one another that easily? If it's so easy, why hasn't it been done yet?" Those are fair questions. The short answer to the first question—Can objects really do this?—is that the idea of using objects makes it possible to seriously consider doing what we described earlier: automating the intelligent integration of different systems from different enterprises upon demand. Without objects, we might as well forget this noble goal, because it will never happen. The rest of this section reveals why I am so certain that this is so.

The short answer to the second question—Why hasn't it already been done?—is that, even with objects, revolutions take awhile. Objects provide a basic framework to enable interoperability, but they don't guarantee it. Only a concerted effort by users and vendors alike over time can bring about such an ambitious goal. I'll spend much of the remainder of this book discussing exactly what will have to be done to bring about this all-important revolution.

Okay, so why are objects so important to interenterprise computing? If you recall, we spent a good deal of this chapter discussing how one object communicates to another *via* a request or message. Furthermore, the format of a request is defined by the interface of the object receiving that request. I said that the really important thing about requests and interfaces is that they isolate the requesting object from anything having to do with the implementation of the receiving object. All that the requesting object is required to know is the interface of the receiving object. Well, if this is true, it doesn't really matter where the receiving object is located, within what application it is running, on what kind of machine it is running, in what language it was implemented, when it was implemented—or pretty much anything else having to do with the particular implementation of the object. In other words, if we use objects, all systems are automatically interoperable at the request level.

Remember the story about Forever Footwear, the wheeler-dealer virtual corporation whose computing system could mind-meld with those of its partners? Let's say that a particular requesting object at Forever is written in BASIC and running their Maine-based PC from within their inventory system. Let's also say that the receiving object is in Brussels on a sales system written in C and running in a UNIX environment. Well, despite all the apparent differences, we can absolutely guarantee that Forever's object can send the message and that the Brussels receiving object can receive it. Even if the Brussels system is completely rewritten tomorrow—in another language on another platform—and moved to Zimbabwe, nothing should affect the requesting object's ability to send it a message, assuming that the receiver's interface has not changed.

This is incredibly powerful. It means that when we enter into a business relationship with someone else, we have a basic mechanism already built into our own business computing systems to interoperate and integrate with their business computing systems. This is true no matter how either system is implemented, as long as each provides appropriate interfaces to its own objects. From a business perspective, this is no small matter. Today, the typical enterprise is a computing island, barely able to integrate and coordinate its own internal computer functions, much less its external ones. The cost of exchanging information with other organizations is seldom even computed, because such exchanges are so enormously expensive that they are seldom attempted.

Of course, there are some emerging service systems that cater to interbusiness communications—global electronic mail and electronic data interchange (EDI), to name a couple. These are already growing like crazy, but still automate only a tiny fraction of business-to-business information flow. They also do little or nothing to integrate the *processing* capabilities of their users.

Having objects everywhere will allow us to vastly expand these fledging information flows from a trickle to a torrent, which will vastly reduce the costs of communicating with business partners and even within our own enterprise. Instead of laboriously repackaging and shipping information in dozens of different formats (all the while arguing over the formats), we'll be able to use one basic format called *objects*. And that format will be set up to automatically send and receive requests from anywhere, regardless of any specifics about the source or destination.

The Telephone Revolution

The ability of businesses to integrate their computer systems almost on demand would have an effect on business roughly analogous to the introduction of the telephone a little more than a century ago; and when Alexander Bell spoke his famous words to his assistant Mr. Watson, Bell changed the world.

Before the telephone, the cost and difficulty of dealing with physically remote business partners was high. Contact by mail was slow, and contact by even the fastest alternative—telegraph—suffered from very low bandwidth and a certain stilted impersonality. It was all but impossible for remote partners to communicate quickly enough to respond to changing business conditions. Strong alliances tended to be local, so people could meet face to face and resolve issues and test out ideas easily. Many businesses did not even bother to work with remote firms unless differences in costs, service, or market were compelling. Those that worked with remote partners seldom changed them, because the cost of locating alternatives and developing new relationships was so high.

The telephone changed all that. Of course, the telephone also had a major impact on local business operations, greatly reducing the time it took for business people to *take a meeting* and, therefore, the cost of communication. But, as long-distance service grew and improved, its most dramatic effect was on remote operation. Why? Because the telephone placed remote partners on an equal footing with local ones. The telephone allowed companies to pursue remote relationships with a much wider variety of partners over a larger range of business opportunities. It also allowed companies to choose among potential partners more easily and to seek the most competitive partnerships available. As a result, there was an explosion in business worldwide and a growing global use of the telephone that has continued ever since. Even when air travel made it easier to conduct global business personally and to rapidly deliver products, it only enhanced the value of the telephone as the great equalizer of communications.

In all likelihood, a similar business explosion will occur when everyone begins using objects for the bulk of their business computing. Objects will allow us to maximize the benefits of the global telecommunications infrastructure we already possess by allowing information and processing to flow unimpeded. Every object and every system built with objects will exist on a peer basis with every other object and object system. In essence, objects will become the common language of all business computing. Objects will allow companies to exchange information quickly and easily, to integrate systems, and to manage their changing relationships—all without the enormous impedance generated by our current generation of monolithic computing systems. And the companies that best understand how to leverage this great potential will prosper. Of course, before this happy day arrives, there are still a few hurdles yet to overcome.

CATCH-23—THE OBJECT ROADBLOCK

So far, I've talked about how objects can help overcome the business computing roadblock described earlier. Objects, I have stated, all have interfaces and messaging mechanisms and, therefore, can easily talk to one another without difficulty. This is basically true but, like most good things, there's a catch—catch-23, to be exact. Of course, *catch-23* is an oblique reference to another great *catch*, Joseph Heller's famous *Catch-22*. In his book of the same title, Heller described catch-22 as a U.S. Air Force regulation that stated a pilot could be discharged only if he was medically insane. Of course, pilots who tried to get discharged by invoking catch-22 were told that their actions were absolute proof that they must be sane.

Well, catch-23 is a little like that. It starts by saying that to be an object you have to have a request mechanism. It then says that to talk to any other object, you must have the same request mechanism as every one of those objects. But, here comes the catch—what if there's no standard that describes request mechanisms? The problem is a little like saying that everyone must speak a human language. This is certainly reasonable, but what language should they speak? If you speak German and I speak French, we have both met the qualification for speaking a human language but that doesn't guarantee that we can speak to one another.

Remember Forever Footwear, the mythical virtual corporation I introduced earlier? In its deal with Just Leggin's', Forever Footwear was able to leverage both companies' information systems to put together a major business deal in just a few hours. The only way that could possibly happen is if the two systems communicated through a common, standard request mechanism. However, without such a standard request mechanism, Forever could build a perfectly good object system, where all the Forever objects could talk to each other but not to Leggin's objects. Without a standard, no one could guarantee that the two systems would communicate accurately unless both of them used the identical object development tool. That, in a nutshell, is my *catch-23*.

Now, of course, Forever and Leggin's could build special messaging gateways between their systems. Such gateways work like human interpreters, translating the messaging language of one system into the messaging language of the other, losing only a minimum of meaning in the process, it is hoped. But such gateways are really just Band-Aids that run against the grain of true interoperability. Forever and Leggin's would have to build such gateways between every object-pair that might communicate, and even that would not necessarily allow them to communicate or interoperate with the computing systems of any other organizations. So, gateways will not really solve our main problem.

The consequences of catch-23 are serious. Companies that can see the benefits of object technology may be champing at the bit to invest in this new approach. However, unless they feel certain that the systems they produce will interoperate and communicate with other object systems, they may not be willing to make that investment wholeheartedly. And if some companies aren't making the investment, then there is less incentive for other companies to do so. Catch-23 again. Actually, the catch-23 problem runs quite a bit deeper. Suppose the Forever organization decides to go back to being a traditional corporation and to focus only on its own internal systems. However, let's say that Forever was considering using objects, anyway, because of their various other advantages.

Now, this strategy would work fine, as long as Forever built everything from scratch with the same software development tool, or was able to buy object libraries from third parties that also used that tool. But, as soon as Forever wanted to look at other object products, it would be faced with the exact same interoperability problem that it had when it was trying to interface to Leggin's'. But, if Forever can build true object applications only with a single tool, we are almost back to where we started—the monolithic system. True, we may have a *better* monolithic application—easier to develop and maintain, maybe with a beautiful user interface—but a monolithic system nonetheless. Forever can leverage its own software efforts but cannot leverage the tools, systems, or information of others. Catch-23, one more time.

But How Will We Manage?

Now, suppose we could wave a magic wand, and everybody would suddenly agree on a single standard object-request mechanism. No more catch-23. Users could then write object computing systems with the object development tool of their choice, knowing that their objects could potentially communicate with all other objects being produced anywhere else.

Are we done? Can we go home now? Unfortunately, not quite yet. Even if we could achieve this utopia instantly, we still have the problem of what to do with all those objects. Catch-24, anyone? Suppose we were now able to create lots of these potentially interoperable objects everywhere in the world. How would we store and retrieve them? How would we move them? How would we find them? And how would we secure them to make sure that they didn't get into the wrong hands? These are big problems that have to be solved before we can have really viable, reliable, large-scale object systems across multiple enterprises.

Consider our Forever example again. When directed to the Forever system, the Leggin's objects were able to figure out which objects they needed to talk to, where they were, and what they needed to say to them. They also knew which objects were secure and how to access them with an appropriate security clearance. All of these activities go well beyond the basic ability of making a request to another object. Each of these various activities is directed toward *managing* the objects we create. This suggests that we need to create a whole new field of endeavor called *object management* if we ever expect to reach the goal we've set for using objects widely in business computing.

OBJECTS AS ASSETS

Another way of looking at this is to realize that our objects will become valuable, reusable resources—in a word—*assets*—to our business. And like all other assets, they will require expert management to maximize their value and minimize the cost of maintaining them. In other words, we will have to invest in and install mechanisms for managing objects, just as we have mechanisms for managing other business assets, such as machinery, employees, or buildings.

This idea of objects as assets bears a little more examination. We know that, when building traditional business computing systems, a company will make a sizable investment in creating software to support that system. But, no matter how successful the new business system is and no matter how important the new software was to that success, very few companies will look upon that software as a true business asset. More likely, the development of that software will be viewed as a sunk cost and, as soon as that software is released, the annual cost of maintaining it will be viewed as an assumed liability. That's because the software probably cannot be sold outside the enterprise, and it can't be leveraged for many other functions inside the enterprise. In addition, the cost of maintenance is expected to rise over time, rapidly discounting any current or future value the software may have.

In other words, from a financial point of view, the traditional IT department in most companies is more akin to the building-maintenance department than to, say, the R&D or manufacturing departments. R&D creates new assets in the form of product ideas, and manufacturing manages those assets to create real salable products. However, IT and building maintenance are simply support services that must be funded to keep the business running—in other words, cost centers.

Reusable Assets

All this changes with objects. Because objects are reusable components of our overall business model, they can be used over and over again in different applications. Every time a given object is used, it becomes, in effect, that much more valuable. And every time an object is improved through maintenance, the value of every other object or application that uses that object becomes more valuable—an appreciating asset. And the cost of that maintenance can reasonably be amortized across all the affected objects and applications.

This picture becomes even more interesting when you consider the movement of objects and object requests among enterprises. In our example with Forever and Leggin's, objects and requests were flowing hot and heavy from one system to another. Every time one of those objects was accessed by another partner's system, it became a valuable part of the business relationship that was being created. This also puts the issue of object *management* in a different light. When I first introduced object management, it was described as a way to keep track of and maintain objects—in short, a solution to a technical problem caused by having lots of objects. But if objects are assets internally as well as externally, then object management is not only a technical issue, but a critical strategic business issue as well.

This also puts information technology in a new light. In the old model, IT was a tactically oriented cost center, providing services to truly strategic parts of the enterprise. But, in our new model, IT has been transformed into an asset development and management center, a strategic part of the enterprise in its own right. In the next chapter, I'll discuss the subject of object management in much more depth. But before I do, let's look at one more issue that will be critical for the business success of object technology.

Get Your Red-Hot Objects Here

Let's wave a magic wand again and give everyone a great set of standardized object-management services. None of us has a real excuse any longer for not building all of our business computing systems using objects. Is the revolution over? Are we done? Not quite. There is at least one more area left to address. Let's assume that the world is filled with jillions of objects and that they are all supported by a full complement of the required set of worldwide object-management services, all running over the *meganet*, our global network. The next questions are how to present these objects for sale to others and what to charge for them.

This is not quite as futuristic or esoteric as you might think. Take television, for example. In just the last 10 or 15 years, we have already moved from no-pay to pay-for-channel and even to pay-per-view television. The stretch from pay-per-view television to pay-per-object business computing is not very far. However, it has massive consequences for the business computing industry.

True to our previous hardware-centric view of computing, computing changes in the past were generally measured in terms of processing units (machine cycles, memory usage, storage, and so on) and electromagnetic storage used. Even today, public networks, such as CompuServe and Prodigy, typically charge by connect time, storage, or number of database accesses. In our global meganet, this CompuServe-style approach won't work. In the meganet, users are connecting to objects and object services, not applications or hardware. The cost of developing, maintaining, and servicing those objects, plus the market value of their information and processing logic, must all be factored into their price.

This pricing problem is similar to any component industry. For example, when Intel or Motorola introduces a new computer chip, what should its price be? It certainly isn't priced solely by the unit cost of the materials or labor that went into stamping out a single chip. Those few pennies wouldn't begin to convince Intel or Motorola to stay in the chip market. Instead, manufacturers must charge a per-unit price reflective of the *perceived* value of that chip in the marketplace. Of course, that price must cover per-unit costs and overall research, management, marketing, distribution, and manufacturing costs—or the chip vendor will close up shop. However, the real price of a chip will be determined by its value as an asset to the customers who buy it and use it to support their own businesses.

Much the same argument can ultimately be made for objects. For the moment, the value of objects is likely to remain hidden in the applications that use them. But, eventually, when objects become widely prevalent, we must decide how we are going to create a true market for objects that includes pricing, delivery, and maintenance. I'll talk more about this interesting subject later on.

A Standard in Time Saves Nine

It should be obvious by now that the object industry cannot truly progress without substantive standards. Object vendors cannot sell objects on their chief merit—interoperability—until there are solid notions about how all objects can interoperate. However, as was pointed out earlier, the usual problem with computing standards to date is that they have been primarily vendor-driven, not industry-driven. Often, standards efforts for a given technology come long after players already have major investments in that technology. Those investments create a substantial disincentive for the players to agree on any single, meaningful, comprehensive set of standards.

One of two outcomes is likely from such a standards effort: One outcome is that each vendor will haggle endlessly over every detail of the proposed standard in order to defend its particular approach. In this case, the standards effort will fall apart or, worse yet, bog down. Each vendor will then claim to be the true standards-bearer, resulting in that old oxymoron: multiple standards. The other outcome is that the vendors will decide to agree to a watered-down compromise, which almost any product can claim adherence to—and, indeed, almost every product will. This kind of standard is really just a marketing ploy for the vendors and not much good to users. It leaves off well before reality begins, once again leaving the field open to multiple de facto standards from individual vendors.

The object industry simply cannot afford to fall into either of those two traps. If it cannot develop a set of meaningful and comprehensive standards in short order, many of the most powerful rationales to induce customers to embrace object computing will be lost. And, as I have pointed out, this will have serious consequences for the business community as a whole.

Fortunately, the object industry has more than a fighting chance to develop such standards. The concept of objects already enjoys a wide spectrum of support from both vendors and users. However, neither vendors nor users have yet made the kind of investments in this technology that would force them to defend and maintain entrenched positions. For the next several years, the window of opportunity will remain open for meaningful standards. During that time, more and more businesses will develop an understanding concerning what those standards are likely to encompass, and by what process they are likely to be implemented. Before that, however, they'll need to take a deeper look at object management—just as we will in the next chapter.

CHAPTER 4

Object Management

ARE YOU MY TYPE?

At the very beginning of this book, I presented the idea that business computing systems should built from component parts, just as every other kind of complex system is built these days. I showed how building computing systems with components would reduce the cost of their development and open up substantial new business opportunities. I then discussed how these business computing component parts, or *objects*, would operate. I stressed the capabilities (predictable behaviors) of individual objects and described the requests that triggered these capabilities by speaking (invoking) their method-names, as described in the object interface. I even hinted at the importance of being able to automatically stuff new chunks of behavior-code (implementation) into each bottle (methods) inside a set of objects, without rewriting any code in the main application that creates and manipulates the objects.

Now, I want to remind you of the three major behaviors every true *object system* must have:

- The ability to define new classes and subclasses of objects at will.
- The ability to create new objects of any previously defined class.
- The ability to send requests among those objects based on their object interfaces.

If this still sounds like a lot of technical hokum, a simple example should suffice to bring it back to earth.

Suppose you create an object class, or grouping, called the *Customer* class. Every new Customer-class object you create from now on will start life with the same state information, behavior (methods), and interfaces (the set of method-*names* plus their *information* requirements) that every other Customer-class object started with. Feel like creating another object

71

class? Let's call it the *Account* class. Again, every new Account-class object will start life with the same state information, behavior (methods), and interfaces (the set of method-*names* plus the methods' *information requirements*) that every other Account-class object started with. For example, let's say that every Account-object has a *ComputeBalance* method on board that gives it the capability of computing its own balance every time it receives a request that contains a *ComputeBalance* invocation, plus all the related information specified in the object's interface (information such as what monetary system to use and the exact hour, minute, and second to compute the balance—a few minutes of extra interest charges could amount to quite a bit on an account amounting to a billion dollars, yen, or pounds sterling).

Now that the two object classes exist, you can create as many Customer-objects or Account-objects as you like at any time; so, create a bunch of both kinds. Ready to use the request mechanism to send requests from an existing object to any other existing object? Good. Pick an object, any object. A *Customer*-object? Okay, let's say that the Customer-object in question has just received a request containing a *ComputeBalance* method invocation plus some information indicating that the balance should be figured in U.S. dollars and that it should be a TOTAL balance of all of the Account-objects belonging to that Customer-object as of midnight on a certain date. What does the Customer-object do? Interestingly enough, the chunk of behavior-code (the *implementation*) stuffed in its *ComputeBalance* method is a lot smarter and a lot more lively than the behavior-code stuffed into the *ComputeBalance* methods in each of the Account-objects. To reiterate an important object concept, though the method-name (interface) is the same, the behavior-code stuffed in the method (the implementation) can be completely different from object to object and from class to class.

Meanwhile, back at your Customer-object. The behavior-code stuffed in its *ComputeBalance* does several things in the following sequence:

1. It deciphers the information that accompanied the method in the message.

2. It checks its own state information to see which specific Account-objects belong to it on the given date and sends a request to each of these authorized Account-objects.

3. Guess what? The request contains the *ComputeBalance* method plus some needed information, such as the *U.S. dollars* information it received.

4. It then sends a "compute balance" message to each of its authorized Account-objects.

A Simplified Example of Object Interaction.

Each Account-object receives its personalized request from the Customer-object and triggers the behavior-code in its *ComputeBalance* method. The behavior-code picks through the object's state information and figures an appropriate balance in U.S. dollars. Each object then sends back the requested balance so that the Customer-object can total them up and display the requested TOTAL balance on the screen or in a printed report of some sort.

If we stick to small, two-class examples like this and don't think about implementation details, it really isn't very hard to imagine how the system works. In your mind's eye, you can almost see the requests whizzing around among the Customer-objects, Account-objects, and other related objects as various transactions or inquiries are performed. No problem.

Well, actually, there *is* a problem and it's a beauty. When you stop thinking small and start thinking about millions of objects divided into thousands of object classes, things start getting out of hand. And when you start thinking about objects on a large, global scale—tens of thousands of businesses each defining hundreds or thousands of classes, creating jillions of objects from those classes, and sending untold *bazillions* of requests among these objects in a worldwide network—well, that's when most people's eyes get glassy and their heads begin to pound.

However, the global scale is *exactly* where things start getting interesting. Think of a telephone network—if it has only a few subscribers on voice lines, it's just a curiosity. Add a few thousand subscribers and it starts to act like an interesting alternative to face-to-face communication. But when you collect a billion subscribers and throw in data, fax, and video transmission, something really viable emerges. Of course, as a telephone system moves from a few hundred subscribers to a billion subscribers, it encounters a whole new set of management problems. These problems don't result from hooking up new customers per se—that works pretty much the same for the billionth customer as it did for the first. The problem has to do with keeping track of all those customers, all their equipment, all their phone numbers, all their calls, all their options, and so on.

It's pretty much the same with objects: As we expand the number of objects and object classes in our object-oriented system, our problem is keeping track of all those objects types, all those objects, and all those requests—and our problem seems to grow exponentially. Even at something less than a worldwide scale, this problem can get quite hairy. For example, consider a set of integrated applications formerly running on a mainframe, but now using objects to run on a large network. At any given time, there could easily be a thousand classes, several million stored objects, and several hundred thousand active objects, with millions of requests flying around among multiple processors and locations, every hour of every day.

The set of issues and problems related to managing objects in large-scale systems is called, appropriately enough, *object management*. I touched upon the subject of object management earlier, but it's time to dive into the deep end of the pool. Object management is a separate subject from object analysis or design, both of which deal with how *individual* applications or closely related sets of applications are best chopped up into useful objects and classes. Object management, on the other hand, deals with problems common to *all* object applications and systems, particularly those of a significant scale.

We could sidestep the hairier problems of object management by creating only very small object systems. Unfortunately, this smaller-is-better approach defeats the true purpose of using objects, which is to encourage reuse of objects and object classes across many applications and systems. If we really want that reuse and the business advantage it provides, we'll just have to face up to the problems of object management as they relate to huge object-oriented systems.

First, some good news: Object management may not be a trivial problem, but it's not an intractable one, either. A life form that has managed to build and maintain a worldwide telephone system, post office, and transportation system in a few generations should be able to figure out how to manage zillions of objects in a decade or two. Also, no matter what kind of management problem you encounter in an object system, and no matter how large or complex that system is, it can ultimately be broken down into something—well—manageable. This truism is valid because every kind of object-management problem can be analyzed in terms of the way it handles three things: object classes, individual objects, and object requests. This insight gives us a great place to begin our detailed view of this very important subject.

A CLASSY DECISION

As I've pointed out, one of the main, new wrinkles about objects is that they give business computing developers the ability to define new types of objects and object classes that can be used and reused at will. Objects enable us to create a computing system that directly represents business components, such as *Customer* and *Account*, which can be reused wherever and whenever the need arises, now or in the future.

Traditional computing techniques and programming languages do not provide any direct support for defining object classes or reusing them. In the traditional analysis phase of a business application development project, software developers often identified business entities, such as *Customer* or *Account*, that they thought of as simple objects. However, during the design and implementation of the traditional application, these half-baked objects invariably would be broken into traditional forms, such as data structures, subroutines, and modules, in which most of their original identity and integrity as objects was lost. This whole process was repeated over and over again, project after project, with little or no reuse of any of the elements created in the earlier projects.

In object systems, however, a strong focus remains on object classes and subclasses throughout the entire design, implementation, and maintenance process. This emphasis on classes changes how software developers look at business computing systems. Instead of worrying about lines of code, database structures, or subroutines, object developers spend most their time defining, implementing, creating, and reusing object classes.

Now, as stated before, one of the main goals of today's object developers is to make use of any object classes or subclasses that have already been defined and implemented. If you can reuse an existing class, you *leverage* all the time that went into designing, implementing, and testing that class; and you *save* all the time that you would have devoted to designing, implementing, and testing the new class. It also saves you maintenance cost down the line.

If a software developer finds it necessary to create a new class, the goal is to create one that is likely to be reused in many other applications. That way, the time and cost of development and maintenance can ultimately be *amortized* across several applications, not just the one currently being built. Also, if developers can take advantage of reusable classes across many applications, the objects created in those applications will be easier to share among applications, not to mention more *interoperable*, a significant attribute that clearly deserves its own boxed definition.

> **Interoperable:** the degree to which object classes are capable of exchanging information and requests within the same system.

A real-world example of interopability? Well, suppose you create a bunch of *Customer*-objects in application *B* using the same *class* of *Customer*-object that you used in application *A*. Because objects of the same class are designed for maximum interoperability, you can be 99.9 percent certain that all the *Customer*-objects you create in application *B* can also be used in application *A*, and vice versa.

In any case, the ability to reuse existing object classes can have a profound effect on how object systems are developed. Many experts already believe that, for well-organized object-computing development projects of significant size, up to 80 percent of the code written is to create and send requests to objects whose object *class* has already been defined and is being reused. Only 20 percent of the code, therefore, represents coding in the traditional sense, and that includes all the code required to create new objects. In other words, *less than 20 percent* of a well-designed implementation written today corresponds to the traditional kind of code normally written with traditional software languages. Furthermore, *all* of the object-oriented code written in an object-oriented software language for a given application usually amounts to about 20 percent of the code required to code that application in a traditional language.

Now, if this fact is true today, in the relative infancy of object computing, think about what will likely be true as the available inventory of reusable object classes grows and becomes more and more available globally. In the not-too-distant future, it will probably be considered archaic to design or code *any* application from scratch. Instead, the norm will be to grab a bunch of business object classes from a gigantic, worldwide assortment available on the meganet, create a handful of new classes that tie the reusable classes together, and—*voilà!*—a new application is born with no muss, no fuss, and very little coding.

This futuristic vision certainly blows a large hole in the rationale of many traditional efforts to improve software productivity. For years, the main productivity goals in software development centered around increasing the lines of tested code produced per unit of time and personpower. This focus on the *quantity* of generated code fostered a considerable demand for programming tools designed to meet this goal, such as fancy editors, design aids, code generators, testing tools, and so on. This industry, commonly known as computer-assisted software engineering, or CASE, struggles on today with a minimum of solid success stories.

With objects, however, improvements designed primarily to speed coding no longer seem very compelling. The significant gains in productivity will be achieved through reuse, not faster coding. Another way of looking at it is, it's not what you *do* that makes you more efficient, it's what you *don't have to do*. Effective reuse drastically cuts down the amount of new code required, eliminating not only the code itself, but also the need to test, integrate, and maintain the code over time. In the object world, CASE will still be around, but its focus will be on managing classes, not generating code.

A Trip to the Repository

Trust me, the next generation of software development tools will primarily focus on reuse. These tools will include cataloging tools to organize *existing* reusable object classes, and design and analysis tools to aid in building *new*, reusable object classes. The main value shared by all of these tools will be to populate and manipulate a central repository of reusable classes, or what object-gurus tend to call the *class repository*. A good definition of a *class repository* is as follows.

Class repository: any facility that keeps an inventory of previously developed classes in a convenient classification system that enables intelligent retrieval.

A class repository can be anything from the developer's brain, to a chart on the wall, to a company-wide database, to a worldwide automated database specifically designed to handle object-class definitions. Over time, as object systems grow in size and complexity, repositories will migrate toward something like the last two options.

The advantage of using a class repository is that, anytime you want to, you can browse through the repository and determine if any existing object class is similar to one that you are thinking of creating. If so, you can check out a copy of the existing object class and reuse it by dropping it right into your object-oriented code—no fuss, no muss. And, of course, if you create an interesting new class from scratch, you can sell or donate it to the repository to be reused by anyone else who might find it useful.

As you can see, this is really very similar to what we do when we go to an ordinary book library. Rather than reinvent the wheel, we look in the card catalog under *wheel* and see what else has been written about the subject. If we know a bit more about what we want, we can search for a subclass, such as *bicycle wheel* or even *alloyed bicycle wheel*. If we're lucky, we'll get a direct hit; if not, we'll check out the closest match and see if it contains any of the information we need.

To push our library analogy a little further, note that there are three main kinds of people involved with libraries: readers, librarians, and publishers. Readers are the ordinary citizens who just borrow books to read when they need some information. Librarians have a more complicated job; they help readers find the right books and, based on their assessment of the demand, order new titles from publishers. Publishers are responsible for finding authors to generate new books based on *their* assessment of likely demand. If a given publisher guesses right, it makes money selling copies of new books to libraries and individuals. For example, if a publisher notices that there are no books on *bicycle wheels*, but high demand for books on *bicycles* and *wheels*, the publisher might publish a title on the subject of *bicycle wheels*, hoping to satisfy both areas of high demand. Of course, publishers also listen to direct requests from librarians and readers.

Our notion of an object-class repository operates in much the same way. Each enterprise maintains a local repository full of predefined object classes already in use in the firm. These object classes will be checked out as desired by ordinary users and developers, who, like ordinary book readers, use those classes strictly in their own applications. Each repository is stocked and maintained by a class librarian, who helps users locate appropriate classes. If our class librarians start to receive requests for new classes, they first check to see if anything similar is already in the local class library; if not, they contact object software publishers and purchase the requested classes, assuming that they are commercially available. Of course, object publishers will try to anticipate this demand, regularly developing, publishing, and marketing useful new classes.

Much like book publishers, each object publisher will probably specialize in a given area—accounting, inventory, data acquisition, graphics, and so on. In addition, many companies in other principal lines of business will probably develop specialized classes that they sell for additional profit. For example, an insurance company might sell its nonstrategic insurance classes to other insurance companies.

Just as book libraries and publishers are now making their wares available online, so, too, will object-class sellers and publishers. Instead of laborious searches through multiple class repositories, our future object developers will have a single interface to all the class repositories in the world, conveniently connected by the worldwide meganet.

An Object Repository Works Like a Book Library.

Would You Like to Interface?

So far, drawing an analogy between book libraries and class repositories has been fairly useful. However, the analogy is beginning to show signs of strain, so let's leave it behind and take a look at some vital issues that affect class repositories and the businesses that will use them.

The first issue to address is *interoperability* among classes. Remember interoperability? The degree to which two classes are capable of exchanging information and requests within the same system? I knew you would. The opposite side of the interopability coin is this: If two object classes are *not* interoperable to a very high degree, they cannot be used together in the same application. For example, if the *Inventory*-object class you have chosen to use does not make use of the same interface format as the General Ledger Account object–class you have chosen to use, the two classes probably can't both be used together. It would be like going to a hardware store and buying a bubble-pack of bolts and another bubble-pack of wingnuts. Even though every bolt is just like every other bolt, and every wingnut like every other wingnut (as objects of the same class should be), if the format of the bolt's threading pattern doesn't exactly match the format of the wingnut's threading pattern, these two groupings (classes) of fasteners cannot be used together.

The need for a high degree of interoperability among object classes suggests that object classes in a class repository must be carefully defined and classified. At a minimum, we all need to know exactly what interface standards each class follows so that we can determine which combinations of object classes will work together. We will also have to know for each object class the other classes that are absolutely necessary for its operation—in other words, its *class dependencies*. What is a *class dependency*? Well, suppose the *Inventory*-class I dreamed up earlier *required* that a certain *General Ledger Account* class be available to it at all times. If the *General Ledger Account* class is around, this class dependency is no big deal. But, if it isn't, we'll have to not only find or generate all the code necessary to create the required *General Ledger Account* class, but also make sure that it is completely compatible and interoperable with all the other object classes already floating around in our system.

It's a little like going to a record store to buy the latest music album and discovering that it's available only on CD. If you already own a CD player, no problem; but if you own only a tape player, then you've got to somehow acquire a CD player—a required dependency—to play that album. This dependency alone adds significantly to the cost and trouble of listening to your new album. It also opens up a new can of worms: You must now make sure that your new CD player will interoperate with all of your existing stereo components.

Dependency problems get quite a bit more complicated when you consider the issue of code maintenance and upgrades. From time to time, of course, a given object class will require either maintenance to fix newly reported implementation bugs or upgrades to add new features. At a minimum, all of the existing users of that class must be informed of the availability of the new version. In addition, some changes to the class could affect its interface or its current dependencies. In that case, every user of the class must be notified and may need to make significant adjustments to existing systems to accommodate the updated version.

No Simple Solution

The problems associated with interoperability and class dependencies are far more numerous than I've indicated. Organizing and maintaining a class is no easy task; a significant amount of work will be required to develop and enforce standards relating to defining classes and documenting their interfaces and dependencies. Otherwise, object classes will not be reusable beyond the scope of a single application, let alone across an enterprise or on a global scale.

A more sophisticated example might give us a better grasp of the scope of the problems. Complex manufacturing systems, such as the electronics industry, must develop and maintain thousands of different types (classes) of electronic parts. A change in even one class of part, if not properly managed, can easily have cascading effects that would affect many other types of parts in ways that are not easily predicted.

Problems like these cannot be solved unilaterally by any single vendor or user in the object industry. Only a concerted effort by a wide range of vendors and users can create the standards—and the standards enforcement process—required to provide a comprehensive system that can support the development and dissemination of interoperable parts. Later on, I'll discuss just how that kind of effort is developing and what its results and impact are likely to be.

IT'S VERY LATE; DO YOU KNOW WHERE YOUR OBJECTS ARE?

Let's assume for the moment that yet another genie just dropped by. This time around, however, instead of just providing us with a convenient genie-in-a-*method*-bottle metaphor, he or she waves a massive, three-fingered hand and every problem associated with creating and managing object classes immediately disappears. Our worldwide class library is now perfectly organized so that we can maximize the identification of reusable object classes. Our class repository is now capable of predicting with absolute accuracy the object classes that will be affected by any change to the design or implementation of any given object class.

Thanks to the genie, we are now free to turn our attention to another problem—the problem of managing the millions upon millions of individual objects that software developers will soon create from our flawlessly interoperable, endlessly reusable classes. How do we store them all? How do we find them when we need them? How do we move them from place to place? How do we back them up? How do we keep the wrong people from accessing them? When do we kill them off? Any one of these concerns could easily become a serious showstopper.

These new problems have a lot in common with the problems associated with managing all the automobiles on all the highways in the world. It's one thing to track thousands of different *classes* of automotive vehicles available today, and the tens of thousands of classes of parts that make them up. However, this problem pales in comparison with keeping track of the millions of *individual* cars on the highway, not to mention the billions of individual parts they contain.

In object jargon, each individual object created from an object class is known as an *instance* of that class. For example, your account at the bank is an *instance* of the bank's *Account*-class, while you yourself are an *instance* of the bank's *Customer*-class. As much as I hate propeller-head jargon, *instance* can be a useful term simply because it is a lot easier to say *an instance of class X* than *a specific individual object created from class X*.

In any case, the really important point here is that the problems associated with managing instances of classes are on a completely different scale than the problems related to managing the classes themselves. For example, the telephone company probably has a few hundred *classes* of customers, but literally billions of customer instances. Also, class management largely comes into play only when we need to create a new class, examine an existing class, or change the definition of any existing class. Even in a complex system, a few new classes may be created every day, and a few dozen changes made to existing classes. This can certainly translate into a significant amount of maintenance activity, but it's hardly overwhelming.

On the other hand, instance management comes into play every time an instance is created, activated, shared, changed, destroyed, moved, stored, retrieved, secured, accessed, and (Whew!) otherwise operated upon. In fact, virtually anytime any instance of any type is operated upon, instance management is involved. Even in a moderate-size system, you're looking at millions of potential instance-management activities per day.

On the surface, this seems like an overwhelming problem. If we consider our projected global meganet of objects, we see bazillions of objects all over the place, moving around, sending messages to one another, and being created, stored, retrieved, and destroyed. It is hard to imagine how any one object-management system could keep track of all this complex activity. The simple answer is, of course, that no *single monolithic* system can. Even if we could imagine the world's largest, fastest supercomputer devoted exclusively to the task, there is no way it could possibly keep track of all the operations on all the object instances going on all the time all over the world. On the other hand, if we don't keep track of all these objects somehow, how can we possibly maintain our global meganet?

It looks like we are going to have to develop an entirely new approach that allows us to manage *instances*, even though they are widely dispersed and implemented on different platforms with different software tools. We have a fighting chance of pulling off this new approach, but we'll need two new concepts to do it: a *common object model* and an *object service*.

A Great Career in Modeling

At the core of every object system is an *object model*.

> **Object model:** a precise description of what it means to be an object in a given system.

An object model includes the terminology used to describe and specify objects, the manner in which an object communicates with other objects, the relationships an object can have with other objects, and so on. If this seems a bit too abstract, think of the object model as an orientation handbook for models, just like the orientation handbook of rules and regulations new employees are handed on their first day on a new job. We all have a general idea of what it means to be an employee, but the orientation handbook spells out exactly what our new employer really expects of us.

In much the same way, you can't really know how a particular object system defines and handles objects until you get a good look at its object model. Even though two systems both use the term *object* doesn't guarantee that the two styles of *objects* have the same functionality; and it doesn't tell you anything about how easy or difficult it's going to be to manage the object systems together.

If you're interested in managing objects, it's very important that all of the object systems you combine together have the same general object model in common. If each system has a completely different notion of how to describe and manipulate an object, it will be exceedingly difficult to manage those object systems collectively. And if you can't manage the systems collectively, you can't really meet your business goal of achieving fully interoperable systems—which is why you need something called a *common object model*.

> **Common object model:** an *object model* that most object systems have agreed to adhere to.

When two or more object systems interact or must be managed together, the use of a *common object model* means that certain assumptions can be made about the structure, capabilities, and interfaces of all the objects involved. Remember the new employee handbook example? Well, a common object model is a lot like the set of government regulations and common practices that standardize the way employees are treated by all enterprises. One beneficial result of this common model of employment is that, no matter where you work, you have certain basic rights, privileges, and responsibilities. This consistency makes it far easier for employees to move among jobs, or for companies to acquire and manage new workers. Otherwise, every new employee would suffer culture shock with every change.

Now, of course, this common model doesn't—and shouldn't—restrictively cover every possible aspect of employment. Employers must be free to offer additional services or benefits, or to require additional responsibilities or qualifications from their employees, as long as they extend the basic employment model without violating it. This common model of employment allows companies to innovate in many areas while still maintaining a viable standard among all companies. The same is true for the common object model. It must be sufficiently detailed to ensure that any system following the model has the same approach to objects, and that the objects can be managed in much the same manner. Vendors of these systems are free to extend the object model into new areas at will, as long as their extensions don't violate the basic model. This flexibility allows specific object systems to evolve to serve new business needs, but within a common framework that guarantees interoperability and collective management of all objects.

A common object model is exceedingly important. But would you recognize one if it came up and bit you on the ankle? Probably not—which is why I'll soon describe the form and content of a common object model in more detail. For the present, though, the following general description should suffice. The common object model must describe such terms as *object, object class, request, interface,* and other crucial object-related terms. I've provided you with a general description of all of these terms in the first half of this book. The common object model, however, must be far more precise. It must describe exactly what these things are, what's required to define them, what they can do, and how they interact with each other. Thanks to the common object model, when vendors implement the rest of the object model, they'll know that they all understand the specifications the same way.

The common object model must also specify certain minimum behavior that each object must possess so that it can be managed collectively with all other objects. For example, the specification might dictate that each object be required to report its class and provide some sort of identifier that is guaranteed to be unique within its own object system, or to represent itself in a certain way for storage purposes. The more complete the description of common object behavior, the more likely it is that all object systems can interoperate and share the same management services.

Whatever the exact nature of the common object model, it's easy to see how important it is to have a common object model among all object systems. The more complete and precise this specification, the more likely we are to meet the basic business objective of being able to manage and leverage our appreciating object assets wherever they may be located.

Service with a Simile

The next item on my list of important ideas is that of a *service* or, more particularly, an *object service*. Generally speaking, anytime one object instance makes a request to another, the receiving object is providing a *service* of some sort. However, if the two instances are strongly related for other reasons, you generally don't recognize this *service* relationship. For example, even though you might consider a taxi a *transportation service*, you wouldn't necessarily consider your *legs* a *transportation service*, because they are closely related to the rest of your body and are, therefore, reserved for your exclusive use (and, of course, the use of small children-objects who leap aboard your foot demanding to ride the horsey).

Your personal automobile is another example. Although it could be transferred to someone else, you probably don't view it as a generic *transportation service* unless you have teenagers in your family. You are more likely to think of your car as an extension of you that simply enables you to travel, rather than an externalized *service*. However, the road system on which you drive—or walk or bicycle—is definitely a service; so is a public parking lot or a gas station. In general, a service is a well-known public entity that, with a minimum of restrictions, provides a function necessary—or at least very useful—to a broad range of potential users.

The object world takes a similar view. If a Customer-instance owns a given Account-instance, that Account-instance is generally not viewed as an object service. On the other hand, an object that manages the movement of any Account-instance from one customer to another, or from one salesperson to another, would almost certainly be viewed as an object service. Actually, the notion of what constitutes a service is really dependent on your specific point of view—what the propeller-heads would call your *context*. For example, if you are sending a letter, you view the post office as a service. In that context, you don't really view the highways or railroads that the post office uses to move your mail as services, because you don't use them directly when mailing a letter—they are *transparent*. In the context of the post office, however, highways and railroads are absolutely critical services with which they interact all the time.

From a functional point of view, the world is little more than a giant set of interconnected services. Depending on your own current context, your set of services is basically defined as all the services you can find and desire to use. However, once you use a service, the service itself can call on any number of other services, and so on. All secondary services are, however, of little interest to you unless you happen to use them directly for some other reason. In our current context, we are primarily interested in services that help us manage instances of objects. By and large, what we think of as an *object management service* (or *object service*, for short) is something that works with objects of all classes, or at least a broad range of classes, and something that enables us to manipulate those objects largely independently of the behavior they derive from their classes.

Take the universal request mechanism discussed earlier; it is an excellent example of an object management service. Like a post office that obligingly transports and delivers virtually any physical object that falls within its size limits, the request mechanism transports and delivers virtually any request between two objects. The request mechanism doesn't need to know anything about the content or form of the request it is processing, or the type, behavior, implementation, or current state of the objects sending or receiving the requests. It simply takes all requests, delivers them, and asks no questions.

It's an important service and applicable to virtually all objects, so I'll be examining the request service itself in greater detail later. However, suffice it to say that it is just one of many services required to manage objects. Next we'll take a look at another important example of an object management service—the *object database*.

Persistence Pays

No computing application or service runs forever; eventually it shuts down or fails. If the objects involved have not been saved somewhere, they are lost. In addition, not every object that an application uses can be active all the time, because active objects live in the high-rent district known as computer processing memory (also known as RAM), a computing resource that's always in short supply. Objects, like office workers, are constantly being shuttled back and forth between the high-rent district of RAM, where they work, and the slum of disk drives and other forms of inexpensive housing, where they rest between shifts. Where do object-instances go when they die? Some programmers speculate that objects never die, that each time they're *destructed*, they come back as brand-new instances. Others say that object-instances eventually retire and move to Florida. But I digress...

The point is that objects move around a lot, which is why services designed to store and retrieve objects, usually from a disk file system, have been around since the early days of object computing. In those days, these services were sometimes called *persistence* services, because they enabled objects to *persist* (hang around) during the times that they are not actively residing in RAM. More recently, commercial versions of persistence services have come to be known as *object databases,* an oxymoron if ever there was one, because objects don't separate their state-data from the behavior-code that manipulates that data. I guess the powers that be decided that the term *object database* had more marketing cachet than *object persistence system* or *persistence engine.* Perhaps the term *objectbase* will eventually catch on. In any case, for the moment, *object persistence system* and *object database* mean the same thing.

Whatever we call it, the general purpose of an object database is to reliably store and retrieve objects as they are *referenced* and *dereferenced* by applications. In other words, when an application starts up, certain objects are activated, or referenced, so that they can process requests. Unless these objects are already being referenced by some other application, two things must happen: They must be moved from disk storage into computer processing memory, and the activating request must be forwarded to them. When all pending requests are completed, the relevant object-instances can then be flushed from active memory and, if necessary, updated on disk. Later references reinitiate the same process.

If all this shuffling around sounds a bit technical, think of it this way: You are in your office, and someone asks you to process something in the Smerdley file. If the file is on your desk, you can process the request immediately; if not, you must go to your own file storage system, locate the Smerdley file, bring it back to your desk, and open it. When you are done and no more Smerdley requests are pending, you return the (possibly updated) file to the filing system. In object-ese, we would say that you just *referenced* the Smerdley file, sent the file a request, and then *dereferenced* it.

What happens if the Smerdley file contains a secondary reference to another document that you must find before you can process the request? Let's say that you want information on Smerdley's finances but this information is in a subsidiary file. The subsidiary file is referenced in the Smerdley file but information about that subsidiary file is located in its own file. While the Smerdley request is still pending, you retrieve the subsidiary's file and look up the required information. You can now dereference the subsidiary file, returning it to storage. Of course, the Smerdley file is still on your desk, because you are not finished answering the request. You now combine the information you obtained from the subsidiary's file with information in the Smerdley file, and finish the request. The Smerdley file is now ready to be dereferenced.

Example of Using a Subsidiary File.

The way we just processed a request to the Smerdley file is almost exactly the way request processing is done in an object system when an object database is available. When a request is made to a particular object, the request mechanism determines if that object is already active in computing memory or in some storage system. If the object is in storage, the request mechanism passes that object's reference to the storage manager (object database), which moves the object into memory. This dereferencing can be continued until the object we really need is brought from disk and activated. Once in memory, the object can process the request. If desired, we can now flush the previously referenced objects from memory and, if necessary, update the disk.

Now, the technical details of this discussion are not really important. What *is* important is that no particular object even knows that it is being stored in a database, that the other objects it references are *in* the database, *when* objects are brought from the database onto disk, or any other operational details about the object database service. In fact, we can pretty much yank out one object database service and stick in another, as long as their basic behavior and interface to other services—such as the request mechanism—are the same.

An object database on any system should be able to store, find, and retrieve any object on any object system anywhere in the world. This set of capabilities enables us to manage the storage and retrieval of objects in much the same way regardless of the object system we are working with, and to move objects from one system to another without worrying about whether a storage system is available. Now, this doesn't mean that each and every object database—or any other object service for that matter—must be implemented in exactly the same way on every system. The only real requirement is that all object services must meet a certain minimum set of standards in order to interoperate both with other services and with broad classes of objects. But we'll deal with this issue in detail later on. First let's look at an example that shows how object services might be used to solve a real business problem.

Customer 54, Where Are You?

Suppose we want to know the location and status of every Customer-object in the world that was last activated before May 15 of last year. We want this information so that we can update it based on some change in government regulations, and we'll assume that all that information is not in one central place. If I can make a few assumptions about our object system and the object services that it has, the information we need may actually be rather easy to find.

First we'll make the reasonable assumption that all Customer-objects can return the date of their last activity when they receive a request to do so. After all, some form of this request was probably specified in the definition for the Customer-object class, and is the same for all subclasses of the Customer-class. In our meganet, this interface definition would be valid for all Customer-instances, no matter where they are located, when they were created, or how they were implemented.

Next we'll assume that every node on the meganet has one or more object databases—object services that store instances of objects. We'll further assume that each object database can browse through its stored objects, and that each stored object knows which object class it belongs to. If a given instance is a Customer-class-object, we'll also assume that the object database can activate that instance and send it our message to determine if its last activation date was before May 15.

Now, suppose we send a request to all nodes on the meganet to ferret out all of our desired Customer-objects and update them according to the new rules. Each node will forward the request to each object database, which will, in turn, forward it to each instance of the Customer-class inside that object database. If a given Customer-object passes the test (last activated before May 15?), it is activated, updated, and returned to the object database.

It may take awhile until everything is processed over the meganet, but our object dragnet is simple and sure. Eventually we will have the goods on every Customer-object in the world that matches our search criteria. Of course, this example is simplistic. Any number of privacy, logistic, and cost considerations would have to be considered before such a global dragnet could be carried out. As a result, most operations over the object meganet are likely to be much more severely qualified.

Still and all, the sheer *possibility* of performing such operations on a worldwide scale opens up a whole new realm of business opportunities. In particular, organizations that are merging or partnering could form virtual *mininets* to unite all or part of their business computing systems for the required processing of their joint operations. These relationships could come and go, or be reorganized at will, all without having to write new code for new systems or rewrite old code for existing ones.

Did you notice that at no time was anything ever said about the *implementation* of any entity on the meganet? The important point to ponder here is that we were able to conduct this kind of operation without knowing the specific features of any subclass of object, the form of storage of any instance, the type of hardware processing the request, the language used to program any instance, or any other such implementation details. In fact, all that was required was that we have a standard interface to the following objects: all *Customer*-object-classes, some basic standardized object management services, and a common request mechanism. We've already covered object classes and services, so let's now take a closer look at the object request mechanism.

CALLING ALL OBJECTS

The power of the object request mechanism is truly the heart of all object systems. If I had to give up every feature of object computing except one, there is absolutely no doubt in my mind that I'd fight to keep the object request mechanism. The main reason for my choice is that request processing enables the various components of our business computing systems to communicate and collaborate at will, while isolating each component from any changes in the implementation of any other. This unique ability to simultaneously support *collaboration* and *isolation* allows object computing systems to respond rapidly, incrementally, and flexibly to changing business conditions without breaking down.

However, understanding the potential value of a universal, global messaging mechanism and actually delivering an operational worldwide object-messaging system are two different matters. A whole host of technical, logistical, business, and even sociological and political issues must be addressed before such a system can become truly viable.

Fortunately, I already know of at least two worldwide messaging systems that have been proven to work over a long period of time and are familiar to nearly everyone: the postal and telephone systems. Most of us are so familiar with these services that we take them for granted. However, you can learn quite a bit that might be useful for constructing a worldwide object-messaging system just from examining these two existing systems.

Please Don't Kill the Messenger

First, consider the fact that the postal and telephone systems are basically content-neutral. The post office delivers pretty much any letter or package, and the telephone system transmits any electronic communication, to anyone anywhere in the world, without needing to know anything too specific about the sender, the recipient, or the contents. Only the address of the recipient, transmittal format, and possibly the address of the sender (for a connection or a delivery notification) is of any interest to either service. In other words, the service requires only the minimum information needed to handle routing and delivery. In fact, isolating the service from any direct knowledge of the sender, receiver, or contents allows both services to specialize exclusively in the areas of transport and delivery or connection.

At the same time, isolation of the message service from the content of the messages also allows the sender and receiver to communicate through any private protocol they choose. In other words, if the sender and receiver want to communicate in Swahili, they can do so, even though they live in the U.S., and no one in the postal or phone system needs to know or care. This flexibility allows senders and receivers to pick any communications code or protocol they choose, based on their desire for speed, convenience, or privacy.

This same idea allows two fax machines or two computers to communicate over the telephone system, even though it was really designed to handle human voice transmissions. If the telephone system needed to know the specific content of the messages it carried, the idea of sending digital data would never have been viable. Fortunately, however, the separation of the message service from the content of the messages allows that service to be used for many purposes never specifically intended, allowing it to grow in value even without making internal changes.

Finally, isolating the messenger from any knowledge about the receiver or sender (except their address) also ensures that message systems operate democratically. Every user, from the largest organization to the meekest individual, gets identical service when he or she pays the same tariff. Whether you are a big corporation handling thousands of letters and phone calls a day, or one person generating a few letters and calls per week, you receive your next letter or complete your next phone call with exactly the same ease and speed.

This democratic aspect of messaging systems allows new users ease of entry into the system. If potential new users had to make some massive up-front investment before they could use the post office or the telephone, these systems would never have grown at the rate that they have, and they would have realized only a small fraction of the tremendous economic impact that they have had over the last century or two.

All Power to the Federation

Another significant feature of both systems is that they can deliver any message to and from anywhere in the world without apparent strain. Drop a letter into any postal box in the world and, assuming that it's properly addressed and doesn't get lost, the letter is certain to arrive at the doorstep of the recipient. Ditto with phone calls. Whether you send the letter or dial the phone from next door or from the other side of the planet, the same addressing scheme works flawlessly.

What is truly amazing is that, when you address a letter or call a phone number, you needn't have any particular idea of where the recipient actually is—it's quite enough to know the address. The message service then gradually decodes the address, bit by bit, passing it to another post office or telephone switch as each piece is decoded. Eventually the message arrives without any part of the system ever assuming full responsibility for its delivery or having full knowledge of the route.

Post offices and telephones seem commonplace now, but imagine what it must have been like to send a message before the days of a generalized message service. Each sender would need full knowledge of the location of and route to the recipient, which he or she would have to impart to a private emissary. In effect, the only people who could communicate would be those who already knew each other and each other's locales very well. Imagine the confusion that must have occurred each time anyone had the audacity to move!

Nowadays, of course, we freely communicate with people we have never met—people who live in places we can barely imagine, let alone know how to find. In many cases, their addresses were passed to us by someone else because someone thinks the addressees might want to buy something that we sell, sell something that we might want to buy, or have some other common area of interest. Although a look at their address or phone number may still tell us something about their location, this information is really completely superfluous to getting our messages delivered.

For example, suppose a teenager mails a letter from a suburb of New York to a suburb of Paris. He or she may never have been to Paris and, in fact, may be completely ignorant of the location of Paris within France, France within Europe, or Europe on the globe. When the letter arrives at the suburban French postal station, the local clerks may be similarly ignorant. All they need to know is whether the intended recipient is local. If local, they deliver; if not, off goes the teenager's letter to that big post office in New York.

In New York, a slightly more worldly clerk reads the country portion of the address—France—and routes it accordingly. This clerk may never have set foot in France, and almost certainly does not know the location and layout of its suburbs. Once the clerk determines that this letter goes to France, he or she never even glances at the remaining details of the address. Nonetheless, the job is performed flawlessly for any overseas address. By the time the letter returns to France, it is treated just like any other letter. Unless they glance at the return address, the French clerks can't tell whether the letter came from the U.S. or from some city in France—and they really don't care. They simply look at the city part of the address and route the letter on to Paris.

In Paris, the letter is similarly routed to the proper suburban substation by a clerk who may have no more knowledge of that place than did the clerk in New York. Only at the very end is the letter handled by someone who actually knows where the recipient lives. Of course, neither the recipient nor the letter carrier knows or cares how the letter actually got there, or where it originated.

What's the secret ingredient that allows this to happen? The real secret behind any global addressing scheme is *federation*. A *federated* addressing system allows the local post office in suburban New York to federate with the main post office in New York, New York to federate with France, and France to federate with the Paris suburbs. The net result is a system where a New York suburb can deliver to a Paris suburb (and vice versa) without either having any knowledge of the other.

Federated addressing schemes allow local post offices and phone companies to virtually guarantee delivery of any missive to billions of people worldwide of whom they have absolutely no direct knowledge. The post office and the phone company can even assure us that we will automatically be given access to people not yet born—just as soon as they arrive and sign on!

Most important, all this message delivery can be accomplished without the need for any sort of central post office that knows every address.

New recipients, new addresses, new post offices, and even new countries can be added to this system with a minimum of fuss. To add a new address or change an existing one, for example, we need inform only the local post office, not every post office in the global system. This ease of alteration and extension allows the system to grow and change easily.

We also don't care how each leg of the delivery route is actually implemented. For example, if the local Paris post office decides to change its method of delivery from letter carriers to robots or carrier pigeons, no one in New York or anywhere else really needs to know. We also don't care whether the mail is delivered in carts or sacks, how much the letter carrier is paid, or whether he or she speaks English. In other words, the basic messaging and addressing scheme is completely independent of the techniques or tools used to implement it.

Buddy, Can You Spare Some Change?

Now, at this point, you might be saying, "Hey, wait a minute. This guy is trying to convince me that the postal and telephone systems are practically identical." Well, they really are almost identical if we view them simply as messengers. Although each has its own unique way of handling messages, both have all the same basic characteristics of a messenger in the sense of this discussion. In fact, any specific differences between the two messaging systems just underline my point. Even though the two systems are implemented completely differently and use different transmittal techniques, they both are based on similar principles crucial to their operation and success.

But, certainly, the most remarkable similarity about both these systems is their ability to adapt to change. Each system continues to operate in much the same way, even though a lot of the technology, logistics, and economics associated with its implementation has changed radically over the century that each has been in existence. In addition, the number of letters and phone calls, the number of users, the number of locations, and the types of message formats have increased astronomically over this same time frame. All of this has occurred without overwhelming either system or causing any basic change in the way its customers interface to its services. Even the founder of the American post office, Benjamin Franklin, could come back and mail a letter today without learning anything new. And while Alexander Bell might marvel at the modern telephone handset, it wouldn't take him long to figure out how to use it.

Eventually we may invent some kind of technology—perhaps some sort of instant teletransport combined with a universal mind-meld—that obviates the need for the type of mechanisms such messaging systems share in common. Until then, we can probably assume that *all* viable messaging systems are likely to share such mechanisms.

So, the fact that both these systems share so many critical messaging features in common reinforces our suspicion that they may have something very useful to tell us about *object* messaging or what I have been calling *request management*. Given the amazing, long-term success of these two worldwide messaging systems, I would be foolish to go off and invent a completely different system to support object messaging. Fortunately, there's absolutely no reason to do so. With a few minor adjustments and enhancements, we can simply adapt the main features of the systems we already know and trust to service our budding object systems as well. All of the key features of messaging systems that we have just discussed fit nicely with what we already know about object systems.

Message in a Bottle

Before I start dissecting the specifics of object-messaging systems, let me reiterate the three main features of existing messaging systems that we'd like to emulate: First, we want to make sure that we can deliver messages among objects regardless of (and independent of) their content or the characteristics of their sender and receiver. This flexibility allows objects to engage in any communications they like, regardless of the underlying characteristics of the messaging system. It also prevents the messaging system from having to respond to changes in message content.

Second, we want to make sure that our messaging service has some sort of *federated* addressing scheme that allows delivery of messages to any object on any collaborating object system. This way, each object system can guarantee delivery of messages to objects in any other system, even without explicit knowledge of those recipient objects or object systems. This will also allow the number of users and locations in the system to grow and change with a minimum of impact on any participating user or system.

Finally, the messaging and addressing schemes must be completely independent of any particular implementation in any given object system. In this way, the implementation of a piece of the system can be changed without seriously affecting the system as a whole. This independence allows new implementation techniques to be added gradually and incrementally, encouraging innovation and improvement.

Let's first examine the idea that an object-messaging system should be neutral to the specifics of the sender, receiver, or content of a message. Well, this is an object-oriented principle if I ever saw one. We can almost think of the messaging mechanism as a sort of service-object itself, taking messages and addresses from other objects as input and having the behavior of delivering each message to its addressee. By this logic, the sender and receiver are also freed from knowing much about the message service; all they need to know is how to package the message and how to address it. The details of deciphering the address, routing the message, and the process of final delivery are all handled by the message service and are of little interest to the sender or receiver. This also means that messages among objects are potentially as private as we want them to be. Any encryption/decryption scheme we care to enforce between sender and receiver is acceptable and has little impact on the underlying messaging system. Senders and receivers are also free to encode messages for reasons other than security—for example, for data compression.

Our second major feature—federated addressing—ensures that we can send a message from any object on any object system to any object on any other collaborating object system, all without knowing anything about the precise location of or routing to that object or object system. In addition, we can easily add new objects and object systems at will, without disrupting the operations of the existing system.

The final feature—independence from implementation—means that we can bring any object system into our messaging domain, regardless of how it's constructed. As time goes on, we can change the implementation of any part of the system without seriously affecting the whole system. The system can evolve and improve as new technologies become available.

Notice that the key to understanding all three of these features of our proposed object-messaging system is that they are all specifically designed to support change and evolution. We can add new types and forms of messages, we can add new objects and object systems, and we can change and improve the underlying implementation of all or part of the messaging system, all without upsetting our global applecart.

Since the whole business idea of getting into objects was to be able to manage and exploit change, this should make us feel pretty good about objects. Since we are building our object-messaging system upon the shoulders of older, proven messaging systems, we can feel confident that it can be built. And, because the principles upon which it will be built specifically support and even encourage change, we can feel confident that our new object-messaging system will be a major tool for meeting our business objectives.

Revisiting the Virtual Machine

Earlier in the book, when I discussed the evolution of the mainframe computer, I described the development of the *virtual machine*. In mainframe terms, the virtual machine was a kind of partition for running individual applications that gave each application the impression that it was the only thing running on that machine. This partitioning allowed the mainframe to share its expensive resources among multiple applications running simultaneously, without the need for any application to be made aware of the fact.

In the mainframe model of computing, the most valuable and reusable resource available was the mainframe itself. In this context, the virtual machine made a lot of sense. However, today we know that hardware is rapidly becoming a commodity like toaster-ovens or VCRs, and that the really valuable resource to be shared is information—and the rules and processes associated with that information, regardless of where it is stored. Therefore, what we really need now is a new form of virtual machine that allows us transparent access to all that information plus its associated rules and processes. This new virtual machine will allow everyone to connect to these resources at will, just as though each of us were the sole user of a giant, worldwide computing system.

Of course, this scenario is exactly what I have been building up to in this book. I challenged you to free your thoughts from the shackles of the old monolithic model of software so that you could move easily through the world of objects. In this brave, new, object-oriented world, the new virtual computing machine is no longer a partition in a mainframe, but rather the global network of objects and object management services that will soon be transparently accessible to everyone.

The new virtual machine is tailor-made to support the virtual corporation. And, just as a virtual corporation constantly reinvents itself by rearranging its parts or components, it can use the virtual machine to rearrange the associated components of its business computing model. Using the virtual machine, the virtual corporation can change its information systems as fast as it can change itself. This is the ultimate in market leverage.

"But, wait a minute," you might be saying. "Am I just supposed to stand around for 10 or 20 years until this global virtual machine is created? No thanks. I've got problems to solve right now that won't wait."

Ah, but remember, Grasshopper, our new virtual machine is not monolithic, as were the mainframes of old. It is changeable and adaptive, and can grow as the technology around it grows. This means that you can create your own virtual machine of objects today within your enterprise and connect them later on to other object systems to create ever-more-powerful virtual machines. Each object you create, and each system you federate with, increases the power at your fingertips—your virtual machine. Whether we ever reach the point of having a true global meganet is a side issue. The real issue is that, with the appropriate object-management systems, we can create object systems of any size or flavor to meet our business needs, and that we can then adapt and integrate those systems readily as our needs evolve.

There is one caveat: To truly evolve, integrate, and interoperate, the world's object systems must be able to share the same object model, the same set of basic object classes, and the same basic set of object-management services. If the vendors and users of object systems can be encouraged to evolve these key features in the same general direction, we will increasingly be granted the leverage necessary to make objects truly useful on a global economic scale. All of which brings us to our next topic: how we are going to set object-systems standards for the world.

CHAPTER 5

The Object Is Standards

THE ROAD TO OBJECTS

So far, I have painted a picture of objects popping up in every computing application of every business in every nook and cranny of the world. Of course, the world is still a long way from adopting objects so comprehensively. However, in recent years, the rate at which object technology is being adopted, or at least accepted, has certainly been impressive. As I'll discuss in more detail in Chapter 7, recent surveys show that a solid majority of information technology executives and professionals view object-oriented approaches as the wave of the future. Their dominant opinion is that, in the near future, objects will be at the heart of most new applications, development tools, and computing environments. In their view, old-style applications, development tools, and operating systems will give way to object-oriented libraries, languages, methodologies, and platforms within the next decade or so.

What is truly amazing is that object technology is a brand-new subject to almost all of the survey respondents. Until quite recently, the vast majority of object-oriented projects have focused on a single application or closely related suite of applications, usually created by a small group of developers using a single, object-oriented language and an ad hoc collection of tools and techniques. In the object history books, the dawn of recorded time probably falls somewhere in the late 1960s or early 1970s, when the first object languages, Smalltalk and Simula, were invented. As late as the mid-1980s, object technology was still largely the domain of a tiny group of cognoscenti—researchers and advanced software developers. Of that elite group, only a much smaller group had any hands-on experience developing large-scale object systems.

At that time, only a handful of tools were available, most of which were primarily languages, such as Smalltalk, Actor, Objective C, and C++, running on a smattering of platforms with a few low-level libraries. Supporting tools for such areas as design and analysis, testing, version control, configuration, and so on were either in their infancy or virtually nonexistent. The tools that did exist were seldom more than minimally interoperable. Until quite recently, therefore, there were good reasons to believe that objects were nowhere near ready for prime time. Conventional wisdom suggested that another 20 years might pass before objects would gain any real mainstream commercial momentum. It was certainly hard to imagine anyone, whether a vendor or user, jumping headlong aboard any sort of object bandwagon.

Nevertheless, by the early 1990s the idea began to emerge that objects might soon become a prevalent, perhaps even dominant, theme in computing systems. Over the next few years, a whole host of mainstream vendors, consultants, and users came to endorse the viewpoint that objects were here to stay and perhaps to rule. And, all of a sudden, it seems, new object applications, services, languages, environments, methodologies, and supporting products are now popping out of the woodwork every day.

Why Objects, Why Now?

What has caused this rapid change of heart? What could possibly drive otherwise sober mainstream vendors and users to abandon their traditional products and approaches to embrace a whole new way of creating and maintaining software, all in a period of less than half a decade? No single, overriding factor has driven this unprecedented revolution. As I described earlier, many interrelated factors have conspired in the last decade or two to create a revolutionary environment in business computing. Changes in business, technology, and the world order have all played their part in turning corporate computing on its collective ear.

At almost any point during the last 20 years, object technology could have been a substantial enabler of change in corporate computing. There is nothing so new about object technology recently that makes it a particularly better solution for business computing problems than it could have been 5, 10, 15, or even 20 years ago. Object technology could have been used productively to build better business computing systems at almost any time since the formalization of the notion of objects in the early 1970s.

In fact, the visionaries of object computing understood the wide-ranging potential value of their chosen field for most of object technology's 25-year history. The basic ideas behind object analysis and design, object programming, object databases, and distributed objects have been around in some form or other for many years. Until recently, however, they remained hidden in the software incubators of universities, think tanks, small startup companies, and the advanced technology labs of large computing vendors and corporations.

Object technology matured somewhat during this long incubation, but not enough to explain its stunning metamorphosis from ugly duckling to swan in the last few years. During that long incubation period, a host of other *new* software technologies, including artificial intelligence, structured programming, CASE, and relational databases, have come of age, albeit with varying degrees of success. In the meantime, object technology remained far from the spotlight, and its adherents labored in relative obscurity.

Whatever transpired to bring objects out of the academic closet and into the commercial mainstream has, therefore, very little to do with any maturation in object technology. If anything, the recent maturation is itself a product of increasing demand.

The Business Computing Chasm

Instead, we believe that the growth of commercial interest in objects is being fueled mostly by what we call the *business computing chasm*, which is an exceptional state of affairs caused by the confluence of two important trends in information systems mentioned earlier. On one hand, revolutionary changes in the worldwide business climate are creating a demand for new types of systems that focus on bringing management information to workers and exchanging information among workers, rather than simply processing operational data. On the other hand, revolutionary changes in computing technology are rapidly moving the locus of the computing infrastructure from the traditional mainframe environment to new enterprise-wide networks of heterogeneous workstations, PCs, and servers.

The rapidly changing business climate is the real driver in this scenario. No matter how hard they try, most business organizations will not be able to maintain or improve their competitive positions without whole new types of software that naturally link together their knowledge workers, business partners, and operational systems into a single, integrated, enterprise-wide system.

Rapidly changing computer technology is, by and large, a catalyst that enables us to keep up with these new business demands. As noted earlier, these two trends are substantially complementary. The new infrastructure is not only potentially less expensive and more flexible, but it also lends itself to placing tremendous computing power closest to (and in the control of) those very knowledge workers who need it most to manage their changing businesses. The possibilities of this brave new union of business imperative and technical improvements are enormous over the long run.

In the short run, however, there is a disconnect between the old business computing order and the emerging new one. The previous generation of business computing applications, infrastructure, and development tools have had their day, but they are increasingly inappropriate as vehicles for implementing the types of computing systems required to fully support the emerging business model. To get to where we would like to be, we must move from the *virtual machine* of yesteryear to the *virtual machine* of tomorrow. Yesterday's machine was designed primarily to run a small set of huge monolithic operational applications on a single, giant machine. Tomorrow's virtual machine will support the flexible manipulation of any number, type, and size of reusable computing components and collaborating services running on a widely distributed, enterprise-wide network to solve virtually any kind of business problem.

But getting from one virtual machine to another will not be an easy transition. In the middle is a great business computing chasm, where yesterday's tools and platforms no longer cut the mustard and tomorrow's tools and platforms are neither ready nor well understood.

Objects and the Business Computing Chasm

Right now, you can almost visualize the vast crowd of business computing organizations milling around at the edge of the chasm as though it were the territorial border line in a great gold rush of some sort. Some organizations have already jumped over the line, sending out advance parties to survey the chasm so that they can lay claim to the choicest ground on its other side. Others are holding back, saving their strength until someone else blazes a trail across the chasm for them to follow.

Many in the milling crowd sense that objects are part of the key to crossing the chasm quickly and safely. The notion that objects are reusable software components, that they can be leveraged across many applications and flexibly configured across enterprise-wide networks, seems intuitive and increasingly attractive. And organizations that have actually *tried* this approach seem to be getting some pretty good results. Most organizations, however, have at best a rudimentary idea of how to use object technology to cross the chasm. Even if they are convinced that objects are probably the right way to go, it's not yet clear to them what the right way to go with objects is. Not surprisingly, this confusion makes most users a little wary. Most are hoping that someone else will leap out in front and show the way—a standard-bearer.

In the past, the average standard-bearer was usually a dominant vendor, such as IBM, Microsoft, or Novell. But, as indicated earlier, that's not really in the game plan for objects. Although it probably won't stop some vendors from trying, in the final analysis, no one can really *own* the object market. Since reuse and interoperability are the key success factors in object technology, it is only through cooperation as well as competition that an effective object market can be built.

For some time now, it has been clear that leadership in the object world will not come from any single vendor, but from a broad industry consensus among both vendors and users. That consensus must actively promote standardization and interoperability among objects, object languages, object services, object tools, and object-management environments.

The OMG: The New Standard-Bearer

As it turns out, just such a consensus is coalescing in the form of the Object Management Group (OMG). The OMG is certainly not the only organization interested in promoting objects and object interoperability and standardization. Older standards organizations and consortia, such as the Open Software Foundation (OSF) and the American National Standards Institute (ANSI), are also working on standards for objects. And newer organizations, such as the Object Database Management Group (ODBMG), focus more intently on specific areas of object technology. However, by almost any definition, the OMG is rapidly becoming the standard-bearer for objects. It is by far the largest and most broadly based organization devoted exclusively to object technology. Its range of standards activities are the most comprehensive, and its decisions are the most widely accepted by vendors and users alike.

For the rest of this chapter and the next, I will focus almost exclusively on the OMG and the efforts it is making to encourage the adoption of object technology and object-technology standards. As you will see, the OMG has taken a different tack from earlier computer industry organizations in reaching these goals. The OMG's approach appears to have substantially accelerated the acceptance of object technology in the business computing marketplace. In part because of the rapid and striking success of the OMG, many users and vendors now believe that significant industry-wide standardization for objects is only a few years away. This is encouraging them to make increasingly substantial investments in object-related products and services, further priming the marketplace for objects.

But, before we discuss in detail the impact of the OMG on the object-computing industry, let's step back a few years and find out how this organization came to be and how it is structured, and then see how it has been going about its job to date.

THE MAKING OF THE OMG

The origin of the OMG as we know it today can be traced back to a series of meetings in 1987 and 1988 among four computer vendors—Hewlett-Packard (HP), Data General (DG), Prime, and Sun. Through these meetings, representatives from each of these vendors discovered that they had a common desire to provide object-oriented systems to their business computing clients. They also decided that their goals in this direction could be better achieved through some sort of cooperation than by just duking it out in the competitive marketplace. Interest in objects was already well advanced within certain parts of these and other computer vendor organizations. Most of this interest was engendered by the same reasons that we look at objects today—the need to create new types of business applications and the need to migrate to new computing platforms.

By the mid-1980s, most established vendors had at least some kind of *skunk works* project going on in a back room somewhere devoted exclusively to figuring out and prototyping what such newfangled applications might look like and how they might best be developed. One of the earliest and most famous of these skunk works was at Xerox's Palo Alto Research Center (PARC). At PARC, Xerox had created a powerful workstation—eventually called the Star—and had used it to develop a powerful, new way of interacting with users. This powerful interface, now called a graphical user interface, or GUI, was originally designed to enable computer novices to manipulate their computing environment in a simple and intuitive way. Steven Jobs, cofounder of Apple Computer, later adapted the idea of the GUI for his revolutionary Macintosh computer; Bill Gates at Microsoft used the idea as the foundation for his now-omnipresent Microsoft Windows.

But the Xerox Star had a lot more going for it than just a GUI. Behind that GUI and everything else programmed for the Star sat a sophisticated object-oriented environment, developed using a brand-new computer language—Smalltalk, which was probably the first language in which absolutely everything was treated as an object. Most of our common notions of objects today—classes, requests, instances—were first implemented in Smalltalk.

The Smalltalk-based environment of the Star gave each worker not only his or her own graphical desktop, but also access to the various components of a typical business knowledge worker's office environment—users, groups, documents, electronic mail, group schedules, work flows, and so on, implemented over a local area network (LAN). Much of what we now take for granted in office systems started out at PARC, implemented as objects in Smalltalk.

Not just Jobs and Gates, but dozens of advanced thinkers at HP, Sun, Prime, DG, and other companies heard about the Star and understood its potential. The dream was that every worker would have a personal Star-like workstation on his or her desk. Through an enterprise-wide network, each worker could access all the resources of the business, and could communicate and share information with every other worker. In the dream, all this could be accomplished without these workers having to become computer wizards: Each would be provided with an intuitive graphical interface modeled after an ordinary office desktop.

The OMG Is Hatched

Unfortunately for Xerox, the Star never went very far commercially. Its custom hardware alone was simply too expensive to be considered a workstation for the average office worker. But that didn't seriously daunt its imitators for long. By the early 1980s, commodity PCs and workstations were already beginning to make the dream begun at PARC start to seem both achievable and affordable in the near future.

At Data General, for example, a project called 902 was started in 1984, intended to give key knowledge workers a Star-like environment, but on commercially available PCs and workstations. Based on what they learned at a series of summer classes at MIT, and on their own experience developing multiuser office systems, the project leaders developed what then seemed to be a futuristic plan to develop something like Star over a network of Windows-based PCs and UNIX servers communicating through a distributed object system.

Daunted by the high cost involved in creating a complete multiplatform object system from scratch, DG looked at a number of other, more traditional alternatives. These included such alternatives as distributing an existing UNIX office system and sharing a relational database over the network. DG concluded that none of these approaches was really up to the task, and somewhat reluctantly went back to its original object-oriented approach.

Between 1985 and 1987, DG decided to devote the bulk of its resources to creating a complete, distributed, object-management system to support 902. At the same time, DG kept its eye out for potential partners who might be able to supply some of the other pieces required to create a full-blown office system.

In 1987, the head of DG's 902 project, Chris Stone, was contacted by Patricia Seybold of the Seybold Group. Seybold consulted to a number of computer vendors on advanced office system strategies, and therefore knew what was going on behind their closed doors. She suggested that Stone might want to contact some counterparts at HP and Prime, who were working along similar and complementary lines. A series of talks, later joined by Sun, led to a loose consortium to share technology. The original idea behind this consortium was rather limited. By putting some money and whatever relevant technology each had in a common pot, the founding members thought that they could accelerate the process of bringing a full-blown distributed office system to market.

HP, for example, was working on an advanced object-oriented office desktop, later marketed under the name NewWave. The consortium thought that this might be profitably married with 902's distributed object manager (DOM) and various other object-oriented elements then under development at Sun to create a complete object-oriented environment. At first, the exchanges were largely technical. Direct cooperation between these normally die-hard competitors was itself almost heretical at the time. Many business details would have to be worked out before such a partnership could be effectively consummated. Before any such deal could be put together, word about the technical discussions going on among the founding four leaked out to others working along similar lines. Soon other vendors asked to participate, and, by 1988, as many as 60 people were showing up at technical meetings. At this point, it was clear that a wide and growing interest in this technology made creating a broad-based interest group increasingly imperative.

In late 1988, Chris Stone, still employed by DG at the time, was named acting executive director of the ad hoc group and given responsibility for formalizing things, hiring an attorney, drafting bylaws, and coming up with a suitable name. By September 1989, the name *Object Management Group* was chosen, the bylaws were written and accepted, and Stone was accepted as its full-time president. By the time the OMG was officially announced in New York City that year, it already had 11 corporate members and a full-time technical director.

The OMG's Standards Dilemma

At its founding, the OMG became the first public, industry-wide organization devoted exclusively to the effective commercialization of object technology. Before the OMG, the only public organizations specifically devoted to object technology were academic or informational, such as the

Object Oriented Programming, Languages, Systems, and Applications (OOPSLA) Special Interest Group (SIG) of the Association of Computing Machinery (ACM).

The founders and early members of the OMG wanted the organization to be much more than a debating society or industry marketing group. At the heart of the OMG was and still is a fervent desire for its members and the object industry at large to agree upon and adopt standards sufficient to guarantee interoperability among all objects and object services, regardless of their source, location, or platform. Many of the OMG's early members already were veterans of the standards efforts of such groups as American National Standards Institute (ANSI) and Open Systems Foundation (OSF). On the one hand, this gave those members valuable experience for charting a course to effective standards. On the other hand, it also made many of them rather gun-shy about turning the OMG into a formal standards organization.

The consensus among the early members of the OMG was that the traditional approaches to standard-setting had proved much too long and arduous to meet their requirements for rapidly promoting object technology. In many cases, the long rounds of the traditional standards processes dragged on for years. Not only was this wearing and expensive for the participants, but it often ended up effectively defeating the standards effort itself. By the time a standard finally emerged, good or bad, it was often viewed by many as already outdated or irrelevant. The results had been similar even when widely different standards-setting approaches were used. For example, some standards were set by trying to agree on a least common denominator among existing commercial implementations. In these cases, bickering among major competitors went on for years over what should and shouldn't be included in a standard.

In other cases, the standards organization itself tried to create the standard by hiring staff and having at it. In essence, the organization itself became a vendor, supplying new technology to its members. Not only did this approach create a new technical and management bureaucracy within the organization itself, but it also failed to stop any of the political infighting. Not only did competing vendors fight among themselves, but they also began to fight with the standards organization. In some cases, this also led to establishment of competing standards groups, another oxymoron if there ever was one.

The OMG's founders feared that, if the OMG used a traditional standards approach, object vendors would go off on their own and develop entrenched market and technical positions that diverged from one another well before any solid standards were in place. If this happened, the final standards would either be ignored or be so watered down as to be effectively useless. This would effectively defeat any effort, however noble, to promote object interoperability, a backbone rationale for adopting objects in the first place.

Fortunately, when the OMG was founded in 1989, no founding member—or any other major vendor, for that matter—had yet established a strong public presence or position in object technology. A window of time existed for the industry to get off on the right foot by agreeing to a set of interoperability standards early on. But the agreement had to occur before competing vendors had developed strongly competitive technical positions that might compromise the possibility of broad interoperability within the industry. In other words, the OMG had to establish its position quickly or risk fighting an uphill battle for interoperability among many potential competitors in an industry legendary for its commercial feuding. Standards were needed, but setting up a traditional standards-setting process would be too slow and, therefore, tantamount to assuring irrelevancy.

The irony of this situation was not lost on the OMG's founders. To succeed, they had to quickly generate relevant, acceptable standards—but without going through a traditional standards-generating process. To solve this apparent dilemma, the OMG had to invent a whole new kind of standards-setting process—and to chart a new course among computer industry organizations. The approach that the OMG finally chose is simple but potentially very powerful. It is a hybrid of earlier approaches, but adds an entirely new twist to the notion of standards and standards-setting activities. Moreover, it turns out that the OMG approach is uniquely suited to the particular nature of object technology and the emerging object marketplace.

Standards for Objects

To really understand the OMG approach, it makes sense to remember that the OMG is in the business of promoting standards specifically for *object* computing—and particularly *distributed* objects—not computing in general. As we shall show, this turns out to be a very important distinction that does a lot to separate the OMG's standards-promoting activities from those of older standards organizations.

To get the gist of this distinction, let's think back to some of our earlier discussions about objects, messages, classes, object services, and so on. First, we defined an object as simply a software component that represented a logical, real-life component in a business system. For example, each customer, account, division, branch, and transaction in a computerized banking system can be treated as an object.

We know that each object represents not only the *information* associated with a given business component, but also all the *behavior* of that component—that is, all the things it is capable of doing. Furthermore, we know that each object is an *instance* of some object *class*, and that all instances of that class share the same behavior. In fact, we know that the behavior for all the instances of the class is defined by a set of *methods* for that class, and that each method may be invoked by sending the object an appropriate message called a *request*, containing the object's name, the method's name, and whatever information is required by the method.

We know that the aggregate of all the different requests that objects of a given class can receive is considered to be the *interface* of that class, because all of the objects' public methods and their informational requirements are contained therein. We also know that when one object (the *sender*) wants to send messages to another (the *receiver*), all the sender needs to know about the receiver is the receiver's interface. Therefore, to describe a potential standard for some class or classes of objects, all we need to know is how to send a request, and what the exact interface is.

Interestingly enough, one thing the sender does *not* need to know to send a message is anything about the *implementation* or *configuration* of the receiver. Which language or algorithms are used to actually implement a method; what machines the receiver runs on; how much memory or disk space it uses; how fast it runs; where those machines are located; how they are connected; and so on—none of these things should mean anything to the sender. As long as it will accept and process the sender's messages, any receiver will do just fine.

This is a huge burden off our standard-bearing shoulders, because now we know that our standards don't have to—and really shouldn't—encompass any implementation details at all. If we have two competing vendors, it is much easier to get them to agree upon an interoperable interface to their products than to agree on almost any standardization in their implementation. In general, vendors get competitive technical advantage over one another by how fast they run, how little memory they need, how reliable they are, what platforms they are on, and so on—all implementation and configuration details.

On the other hand, vendors seldom get much mileage out of saying things such as, "My programmatic interface is better than your programmatic interface." Very few users would understand such a distinction, and fewer still would care very much. However, one thing users almost always care about is whether a vendor's new product will interoperate with other products already on the market or coming soon. If the answer is no, it almost always will hurt the acceptance of the new product and the technology it is based on.

In general, vendors have a lot of good reasons to agree on standards for interoperable interfaces and very little reason not to. Moreover, the faster they can agree on these interfaces, the less work they will have to do later to retrofit their implementations to the standards. But, if this is true, why haven't vendors done this sort of thing in the past? Why has it been so hard to set standards before? And why should it be any easier for objects?

One big difference is actually very simple. When we begin to develop a traditional monolithic software system, one of the *last* things we think about is the interface. The interface to a traditional system is usually defined after the system is completed, and is very specific to the way that system was implemented. Given this, no vendor wants to commit to a specific interface until the bulk of its development work is complete, and no one wants to change an interface that it has already defined. But, when we begin to develop an object-oriented system, one of the *first* things we consider are the interfaces. After identifying the likely objects, we begin to define their interfaces because we want to keep the objects *implementation-independent*. No object needs to know anything about the implementation of any other, but they certainly need to know each other's interface—and this interface should change as little as possible as the system is actually being implemented.

So, in the object world, each vendor needs to know his or her interfaces well in advance of implementation. Also, a commitment to a given interface standard is not a commitment to a given implementation. Long after a given object-interface standard has become hoary with age, vendors can continue to provide new and improved implementations, just as auto manufacturers can provide new engines, brakes, or other components without altering any of their industry-standard interfaces.

OMG's Nonstandard Standards

All of this has played very well into the standards-promoting hand of the OMG. Some members may at first have looked at the OMG as yet another standards battleground. However, all have seen that, within the OMG, any traditional notion of battling over standards really serves nobody's purposes—least of all, their own. In the object world, it actually makes sense for any member to submit object interfaces for possible standards well before any significant investment has been made in actual implementation. This also means that it makes more sense for all parties to compromise over object-interface standards than to duke it out over a protracted period. It is much better to get this stuff out of the way early, and then go out and compete on the quality of implementation and service rather than on interfaces.

Now, of course, this doesn't mean that some members won't fight vociferously over every detail of a proposed standard while it is being considered. After all, each member is likely to have to live with the standardized interfaces for a long time, and wants to make sure that nothing in them will run counter to his or her own current or potential object product strategy. However, once all proposals are out on the table, it is really to everyone's best interest to agree on something quickly.

At the OMG, this has turned the standards-generating process upside down compared to the standards-setting efforts of earlier groups. In fact, the drive for early adoption of object standards is so powerful that the OMG has been able to harness and direct it toward demonstrable results faster than any previous organization. The final irony is that the OMG has been able to gain a stellar reputation for rapid standard-setting, *even though the OMG itself does not officially set standards.* Yes, you read the last sentence correctly. According to the OMG's charter, the organization does not formally set or enforce standards; it simply promotes their general promulgation and industry-wide acceptance. The OMG is in the business of encouraging the emergence of what the software industry calls de facto standards (unofficial suggestions that become standards *in fact* if not in the official record books). In essence, the OMG evaluates the submissions it receives that describe interfaces for various interesting objects and object services, and then the OMG encourages its members to vote on which ones to recommend to the industry at large.

In theory, no one—not even its members—has to follow any one of the OMG's recommendations. None of these recommendations is, officially, an industry standard. Strictly speaking, anyone who does endorse an OMG recommendation is doing so entirely on their own. And, at least so far, there are no *standards police* in the OMG to force adoption of its recommendations, or even to say if a particular purported implementation of one of its recommendations actually conforms to its recommendations or even works at all.

At first blush, it would seem that the OMG has no real teeth and is likely to produce weak standards that nobody will adhere to. However, nothing could be further from the truth. Due to the nature of the object marketplace we just described, the OMG generally can rely on the fact that most vendors can't generate any advantage by opposing its recommendations, and nearly all vendors will benefit by endorsing it as soon as possible. In fact, Microsoft's Object Linking and Embedding (OLE) specification is one of the few notable exceptions to this general rule in the past two or three years.

The truth is that most reasonable OMG recommendations soon become de facto standards, if not technically de jure (legally enforceable) standards. Ironically, this situation frees the OMG from having to worry about the political machinations that have plagued and delayed standards-setting efforts elsewhere. As a result, the OMG can adopt pretty much any structure or process it likes to hasten the agreement upon object and object-service interfaces, without being chastised for not following a highly formalized standards-setting process. As long as the OMG's process is basically unbiased and reasonably thorough and professional, its recommendations can enter the public domain as quickly as the OMG's staff and members can realistically usher them along.

All this allows the OMG to walk and talk like a standards organization, but also to avoid much of the inertia generally associated with actually being one. With this in mind, let's now take a closer look at what the OMG has accomplished in the last few years, and how it is organized.

THE OMG: ARCHITECTING THE FUTURE

Shortly after the OMG's founding, one of its first technical projects was to compile a document known as the Object Management Architecture (OMA) Guide. This document, which is updated regularly, is intended to act as a guiding hand for everyone participating in the OMG, and particularly as a reference model for those who are submitting technology to the OMG for evaluation.

The creation of the OMA and the publishing of the OMA Guide was a major step for the OMG and the object industry in general. Up until that time, there was no standard set of terminology and reference models by which different vendors could describe their competing (or collaborating) object systems. Instead, each vendor had developed its own object architecture, using different terms for the same things or, worse yet, the same terms for different things.

In the days before the OMA was defined, what one vendor meant by the term *object*, or *class*, or *request* might differ considerably from the definitions of another. This meant that anyone trying to evaluate and compare two or more systems would have a hard time sorting out their similarities and differences. Two very similar systems could be described quite differently, and two very different systems could be described similarly.

The OMG realized that this kind of problem, if not addressed, would act like a plague on the object computing industry at large, and it would be murder for the OMG itself, which has been and will be evaluating hundreds of technology proposals from scores of vendors over a multi-year period. By providing the OMA and OMA Guide, and suggesting that technology submitters follow its structure and definitions, the OMG was able to head off a "terminology war" among it submitters—and in the object world in general—that might end up seriously slowing down its evaluation and recommendation processes.

If the OMA helped accomplish only that, it would be worth its weight in golden objects. However, the OMA is also useful in another very important way: It has provided the foundation of a technical road map for how the OMG itself will operate to set standards in the object computing industry. The OMA sets the basis for object standards by dissecting the architecture of all object systems into a few major components. By systematically encouraging the development of standards for each component that the OMA defines, the OMG will ultimately provide a complete set of standards applicable to virtually any object system.

Object Systems Made Simple

The OMA divides all object systems into four main components:

- Object Request Broker (ORB)
- Object Services (OS)
- Common Facilities (CF)
- Application Objects (AO)

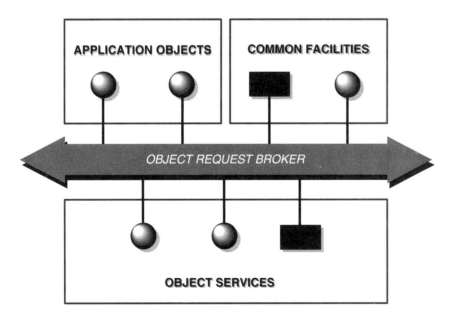

The OMG Object Management Architecture.

To this list, the OMG added two components that I'll discuss in detail later in this section:

- Common ORB Architecture (CORBA)
- Common OS Standard (COSS)

Right now, a thumbnail sketch of each piece of the puzzle should suffice just enough to indicate how it fits into the OMG's overall activities. The first two components—the Object Request Broker and Object Services—provide the guts of the object system, the infrastructure that allows objects to exist, to send and receive messages, to move around within the system, and so on. The next two—Common Facilities and Application Objects—deal with the ways that end users actually *see* object systems. In other words, what is presented to end users in everyday applications and utilities.

In the OMA, the ORB is clearly the center of attention—all the other components use it to communicate among each other. In fact, the ORB is nothing more or less than the universal messaging system discussed earlier. Like a kind of universal object highway, messages can flow through the ORB from any object to any other object, regardless of the size, state, location, or implementation of the respective sender and receiver.

Every object system has some kind of ORB, even if it allows messages to be sent only among objects implemented in a single language within a single application. Without a universal standard for all ORBs, however, objects implemented or running on different systems cannot send and receive requests without building explicit gateways between each pair of different systems. In other words, no matter what other standards are developed, objects won't be able to interoperate easily unless there is a well-accepted standard for ORBs. As a result, it became obvious to the OMG early on that, to be really successful, much of its initial standards efforts would have to be focused on the ORB component of its architecture. In fact, the OMG spent most of its first two years working primarily on standards for the ORB, eventually coming up with what is called the Common ORB Architecture, or CORBA.

We'll discuss CORBA and its potential impact on business computing environments in more detail later on. It is enough to say here that objects communicating through a CORBA-compliant ORB should be able to send and receive messages among any other objects communicating through a CORBA-compliant ORB. Even if two objects were each implemented and run on a different system, and even if each of those systems uses a different CORBA-compliant ORB, the basic standards in CORBA should guarantee that those two objects will still be able to communicate through messaging.

The second major component of the OMG's OMA is Object Services. As discussed earlier, an object service is simply some software designed to provide a particular set of operations applicable to broad classes of objects. For example, a given object service might store and retrieve objects, or it might manage relationships among objects, or it might protect objects from unauthorized access by other objects. The Object Services are the key to expanding the functionality—and interoperability—of objects beyond the simple request management capabilities of the ORB. Consider a security system for objects; such a system would be of very limited value if it worked on only one platform. To be truly useful, it would have to interoperate and even federate with security systems running on other platforms.

A similar conclusion can be reached for virtually all other Object Services. This makes it clear that, having first defined a standard for ORBs, the OMG would then have to focus its attention on defining interoperability standards for key Object Services and a framework for defining Object Services in general. In fact, since the announcement of CORBA, work in the Object Service area has been the major technical activity for the OMG. More than a dozen key services have been defined, and a road map and timetable for attacking these has in turn been established. We'll discuss the most important of these services and their likely impact on business computing later on.

The third component of the OMA—Common Facilities—has only recently become a major activity for the OMG, but it is potentially a very important one. Like an Object Service, a Common Facility provides a specific set of functionality common to many applications, but, in this case, visible primarily to applications and end users rather than all objects in general. Examples include such things as database access, print queues, compound document facilities, graphical desktops, system configuration tools, help facilities, agent task facilities, application linking, and so on.

There are many reasons for the OMG to encourage standardization of such Common Facilities. For one thing, facilities that are directly user-visible are normally better used and accepted, and less expensive to implement, if they operate similarly across various applications and different platforms. For example, there should probably be only one basic way for systems to handle the human interface to *browse* relational databases. This capability would not only ease the learning curve of users, but would also simplify the development, documentation, and training requirements for vendors introducing new products.

In other cases, a Common Facility makes sense *only* if its use and behavior are standard and predictable across all applications and platforms. For example, consider a user who wishes to send someone a document that has been built with a compound document editor. The user certainly hopes that the compound document will be displayed to the receiver in the sender's intended format, even if it is being displayed from within a different program on a different platform than that which the sender used to create it. Emerging documentation standards like those supported by SGML (Standard General Markup Language) are making their presence felt with a vengeance, and will likely receive additional support in the months ahead.

The last major piece of the OMA is the area of Application-Objects. These refer to all of the objects that vendors, independent software developers, and end users are likely to develop as they create their industry- and enterprise-specific applications. For example, there will be Application-Objects for office applications, for graphics applications, for knowledge-based systems, and for specific vocational disciplines— banking, insurance, retail, financial, manufacturing, and so on.

While the OMG intends to get directly involved in the standardization efforts surrounding the ORB, Object Services, and Common Facilities, its position in respect to Application-Objects is a bit more ambiguous. The OMG does not intend to internally evaluate the relative merits of various Application-Objects, but it does have an interest in making sure that these objects make use of OMG-endorsed services and facilities. At a minimum, the OMG's direct activities in the Application-Object area are likely to remain at a low level until more of the Object Services and Common Facilities are defined.

For this reason, the OMG is encouraging the activities of other organizations specifically devoted to particular industries that will independently develop industry-specific Application-Object standards, while promising to adhere to OMG-endorsed Object Services and Common Facilities. Examples of such groups currently include the Petroleum Open Software Corporation (POSC), the Network Management Forum (NMF), and Open Geographic Information Systems (OGIS).

May The Task Force Be With You

Even without getting directly involved in the Application-Objects area, the OMG clearly has an enormous set of tasks cut out for it in covering the other major pieces of the OMA. Given this, one could easily envision the OMG housing a staff of dozens, if not hundreds, of technical staff, busily soliciting and evaluating proposals for the membership to consider. But, in fact, the OMG operates on a tight budget—financed almost exclusively with dues—that can support only a rather small staff. It is true that the OMG's staff has grown modestly since its founding, as more and more members join and thereby contribute the dues necessary to support said staff. However, even if the whole staff of the OMG were exclusively devoted to supporting its technical activities, it would hardly be enough to cover its proposed waterfront.

In reality, only a few of the OMG's small staff are directly involved in technical matters—the majority are in support marketing and administrative functions. If that's the case, how is the OMG able to cover so many areas of technical concern so effectively? The answer is that the OMG staff acts primarily to coordinate the activities of member volunteers, who do most of the substantive technical work. In other words, the OMG gets most of its important technical work done for free.

According to the OMG's bylaws, all activities are formally reviewed and sanctioned by its Board of Directors (BOD), itself a volunteer group. Day-to-day technical activity in the OMG falls under the auspices of the Technical Committee (TC), a body of volunteers formally chartered as *consultants* to the BOD. The TC has been holding regular meetings every six to eight weeks since the founding of the OMG. Any OMG member or invited guest can attend a TC meeting, but only OMG corporate members (the highest membership category) can vote—one corporate member, one vote. Most corporate members participate regularly, with the larger ones often sending several representatives to each meeting—all are volunteers.

The TC initiates all technical activities, including developing Requests for Proposals (RFPs) for object specifications, and developing and publishing such documents as the OMA Guide. And, ultimately, it is the TC that puts its stamp of approval on the specifications that the OMG will endorse, subject to the formal approval of the BOD. However, the TC does not try to do all of its many activities as a single body. At a minimum, this would prove unwieldy, given the TC's sheer size. More important, working directly on each project would cause the TC to serialize its activities, severely slowing down its progress.

As a result, the TC commonly delegates most of its day-to-day work to various Task Forces (TFs), also composed of volunteers. Each TF is given a charter and mission with expected deliverables, and then left pretty much alone to have at it. In practice, this means that those TC members most interested in a given subject area will likely join the appropriate TF for that subject and devote most of their time and effort there. Besides relieving the TC of day-to-day work, the TF system has the effect of concentrating the technical *best of breed* from within the OMG's members on each area of technical focus. Also, the TFs have looser voting, participation, and process rules than the TC. Anyone from the OMG can come, anyone can vote, and even outside people can be invited in as full-fledged TF members if this makes sense.

The TF system, which we will describe in more detail later, has allowed the TC to pursue a wide agenda without getting bogged down. In the first few years of the OMG, the TC was simultaneously developing technology specifications for an overall Object Model, the Object Request Broker, and a number of important Object Services. The results of these activities will be detailed in the next chapter.

In addition to its TFs, the OMG TC can also charter any number of Special Interest Groups (SIGs). In recent years, there have been special interest groups for Object Analysis and Design, Smalltalk, and Graphical User Interfaces. The SIG system allows the OMG to recognize the importance of certain areas for study and information exchange, without making any direct or implied commitments as to when or if these areas might be amenable to more formal evaluation and recommendation by a Task Force. If the SIG generates sufficient interest or output, the TC may then decide that it should create a new Task Force for that area.

Hark the Heralds

Eventually, each Task Force completes its evaluation process and makes a recommendation to the TC. The TC then casts its vote and, after a year or more of hard labor, a new OMG adoption of technology has been born. By this time, most of the cognoscenti of the object industry are probably well aware of the outcome and are already making their own strategic adjustments accordingly. However, most of the computing industry at large has yet to hear about the OMG's adoption, much less digest its importance.

We all know that the most beautifully specified standards recommendation becomes useful only when it becomes well known. Many press releases, many seminars, many product introductions, and many trade shows must be completed before the new standards recommendation is truly understood and accepted by the broad mass of computing industry organizations and professionals. The management staff at the OMG is responsible for getting the word out to the world. While the Technical Committee is busy formulating its recommendations for worldwide object computing standards, the marketing arm of the OMG management is preparing to herald these recommendations from rooftops all around the globe. As we leave our discussion of the OMG behind, I want to make certain that its important missionary work has not gone—well—unheralded.

Actually, marketing has been much more than an afterthought at the OMG. The heralds have been busy since the OMG's founding because the OMG is one of the first organizations of its kind to view marketing as essential to its mission. By their nature, most standards-oriented organizations are technology-driven. That not only means that their primary mission is to produce technology, but also that they are run by technologists. This generally means that such functions as marketing are viewed as secondary—something you do only after you have got the technology right.

The founders of the OMG, however, had observed that this after-the-fact approach to marketing didn't work very well. It meant that when your standard came out, you had to start climbing the industry acceptance hill from the very bottom. By the time you started to build some momentum, so much time had passed that your standard was no longer timely. The OMG decided on a different tack. Almost from day one, they began a marketing campaign to establish an awareness of the OMG and, by extension, the object technology industry. The OMG's third employee was a marketing director who got right to work. Through a series of press conferences, press releases, articles, and presentations, the OMG put out the word that objects were good and that the OMG was good for objects.

Actually, that was just the packaging of the message. The message inside was a little more complicated and sophisticated than that. It said that object technology was important, that it encompassed a lot of other technology, that it was here to stay, and that it would eventually change the way that the world looked at computing. It also said that the OMG was the focal point for objects, the place to go to influence the direction of object technology or to just find out about it. Getting this message across was a key part of the OMG's early overall strategy. By establishing the importance of object technology early on, the OMG could define itself as its standard-bearer. This would attract new members and prime the general public for accepting or at least recognizing the standards that the OMG would eventually generate.

Of course, much of this message was met initially by skepticism, particularly by the press. New organizations and alliances of computer vendors are announced all the time, and everybody claims to have a solution to the computing equivalent of world hunger. The bane of every computer industry news reporter and analyst is to have to sit through another of these lofty but often toothless pronouncements.

In the OMG's case, however, much of this was overcome over time by its fast-track process. Within less than a year of its founding, the OMG was already issuing Requests For Information (RFIs) and RFPs, and its membership was growing rapidly. When it went to the press again, ears began to perk up and listen. As a result, by the time the OMG issued its first recommendations, it had already established itself in the public eye as the focal point for objects and objects standards. By the time the OMG issued its first standard, another important part of the OMG's marketing strategy began to kick in. As we have discussed, the OMG evaluates and recommends only specifications based on already (or soon-to-be) commercialized products. This product tie-in is important for two reasons: First, it tends to validate immediately the specifications that the OMG has recommended—there is already at least one product on the market that does what the OMG suggests. This validation gives the OMG a big leg up on other standards groups, which often wait years for someone to implement the standards they have promulgated.

Second, it creates a tie-in between the marketing of the OMG and the marketing of the products that meet its specifications. In other words, vendors who endorse OMG recommendations and claim to follow them are likely to say so in their advertising and public relations, further adding to the recognition and legitimacy of the OMG.

Another tie-in that the OMG has used effectively has been to reach cosponsoring agreements with other industry standards organizations, such as X-Open, UNIX International (UI), and Open Software Foundation (OSF). In the past, such standards organizations as the OMG have generally either competed with other such organizations or else found a separate sandbox to play in. Instead, the OMG has cooperation rather than competition or separation with other organizations in the object arena.

For example, the OMG has had an agreement with X-Open since 1990 to cosponsor the OMG's adoptions. This has relieved X-Open of the thankless task of trying to duplicate the OMG's efforts in the object arena, while further broadening the reach and expanding the credibility of the OMG at no additional cost. The OMG's efforts to market itself and object technology have gone well beyond public relations and alliance-building. The OMG also has its own regular periodical, *First Class*, which provides news and views about the OMG and its activities. In addition, the OMG standards and technical papers are published and distributed worldwide. This book and others in this series are also products of the OMG's fast-growing publication efforts.

The OMG has established a publishing relationship with John Wiley & Sons, the prestigious publisher of many professional books, whereby the OMG and Wiley work together to bring to market such books as this one, the standards and technical papers, reprints from SIG groups, and books on object technology by various authors that the OMG and Wiley believe make important contributions to object technology. This ongoing effort is important in bringing critical and important information to the practitioner's world.

By far, the largest and best-known promotional effort related to the OMG has been Object World, its annual trade show. Object World, run in partnership with IDG World Expo, a large computer trade-show producer, started as an annual event in San Francisco in the summer of 1991. It has since grown to include annual satellite shows in Boston, London,

Tokyo, Sydney, and Frankfurt, and is now, by far, the largest trade show devoted to commercial object technology.

Object World is run as a for-profit subsidiary of the OMG, itself a nonprofit entity. However, while the OMG does not benefit financially from the highly successful Object World, the impact that this popular trade show has had on the OMG's visibility is undeniable. Every year, tens of thousands of end users, consultants, independent software vendors, and computer industry press—many previously new to objects— have been exposed to object technology and the OMG through Object World's many seminars, workshops, presentations, award programs, and, of course, vendor exhibits.

It is at Object World, not surprisingly, that many vendors choose to announce and to demonstrate their new OMG-compliant products. In some cases, this has gone beyond showing individual products. Increasingly, cooperating Object World vendors are using the show as a demonstration site—they hook up their various OMG-compliant object systems together to show how readily they can interoperate and federate. This generates additional publicity—and credibility—for the OMG and its standards-setting efforts. These many efforts have contributed mightily to the phenomenal growth in the OMG's visibility, acceptance, and effectiveness since its founding only a few years ago. The OMG has certainly profited handily from the recent tidal wave of interest in object technology, and, as we have seen, it has just as certainly been one of the primary promoters of that tidal wave as well.

Over the next few years, the OMG will expand its marketing efforts to include more information specifically targeted to end users of object technology. This change in focus reflects the fact that the market is maturing, and more end users are looking for "harder" information about products, services, and standards that will be used to make buying decisions. And, of course, as the OMG actually produces more standards adoptions, there is more such information for it to communicate.

On that note, it's probably time for us to take a deeper look at how the OMG actually evaluates and endorses technology. No matter how well it is marketed, at the end of the day, the OMG will gain real respect and adherence only if its recommendations make real technical sense to real vendors and users. So, let's next take a look some of the OMG's accomplishments in the arena of technical standards for object technology, and discover how the OMG has done it.

CHAPTER **6**

A Standard in Hand

Leading vendors traditionally have resisted creating and adopting consensus standards early in a technology's commercial life cycle. At that point, they are primarily focused on developing a competitive product line and carving out their own market share. Negotiating standards with competitors is way down on their priority list. Later, when the marketplace has matured and commercial winners and losers have largely been accounted for, the dominant vendor's product specifications tend to become the de facto standard. Microsoft's Windows is a recent example of this kind of behavior. However, when no vendor dominates, the industry continues to duke it out, with different vendors trotting out competing, and often incompatible, approaches that aren't really standards of any sort.

In the last chapter, I described how and why the object technology industry appears to be overcoming this traditional pattern and is successfully generating widely adopted standards early in its commercial life cycle. As I pointed out, this pattern is being overcome largely because vendors have come to realize that standards for objects—standards based on *interfaces*, not implementations—don't box them in the way traditional standards do, and can aid them in their own development and marketing plans.

In addition, vendors anticipate that customers of object technology are going to expect and demand a high degree of interoperability and reuse among different object implementations. That kind of interoperability and reuse can be realized only if the interfaces between different object products are standardized. Object vendors who don't support serious standard-setting efforts risk being left behind by customers who flock to vendors who do. As indicated in Chapter 5, this natural momentum toward standards has been successfully exploited by the Object Management Group (OMG). The OMG has been able to generate significant, broadly supported standards well before any vendor has carved out a significant position in the object market. OMG's efforts have increased the credibility of object technology in the eyes of potential users, and therefore their commitment to it, even before objects themselves have been widely deployed.

As users' commitment to object technology grows, vendors are willing to invest more money in developing new object-oriented products and services—and more products and services trigger a greater need, incentive, and support for developing standards. The unfamiliar reversal of the traditional standards timeline—a major push for standards by vendors and users *before* the marketplace matures—is a welcome variation on a hackneyed theme. The OMG hopes to perpetuate this theme because that organization is really in the process of creating a giant bandwagon to fuel the acceptance of object technology. The OMG bandwagon also hopes to highlight the importance of the standards-setting process until objects are well entrenched in mainstream computing. But a bandwagon left unattended can be a contrary vehicle. The OMG is not simply free to sit back and ride the wave of enthusiasm for objects and object standards; it must quickly and consistently deliver and popularize specifications for potential standards, or watch its bandwagon wobble to a halt.

In the last chapter, I discussed in very general terms how the OMG is structured and how it helps to create and popularize a standard. In this chapter, I'll describe how that process actually creates useful standards before a maturing market can render them moot. And, to demonstrate exactly what this has meant in practice, in an upcoming section titled "The Standard Story," I'll take a closer look at the Common Object Request Broker Architecture (CORBA), the OMG's first widely accepted standard and a linchpin of its standards-setting strategy.

THE LEAN, MEAN, STANDARDS MACHINE

In the last chapter, I pointed out that the OMG promotes standards by endorsing technical specifications from among competing submissions provided by its members. Members normally supply these submissions in response to formal Requests For Proposals (RFPs) issued by the OMG's Technical Committee (TC), with approval of the Board of Directors (BOD).

I also stressed that the TC normally delegates most of the ongoing work in each adoption area to a Task Force (TF). This delegation streamlines each individual adoption process and enables several adoption activities to occur in parallel. Each TF can then focus exclusively on a single subject area, while the TC oversees and coordinates their activities without abandoning its own pursuit of the broader OMG technical agenda defined in the Object Management Architecture (OMA). The formal process that leads to an OMG adoption of technology and (it is hoped) a widely accepted set of standard specifications essentially begins when the TC creates a TF and develops a charter for it. The TF shepherds the adoption process along until it finally makes a recommendation to the TC to formally endorse a single specification.

In theory, the TC can decide to create a Task Force anytime for any reason. However, the various TFs, like the TC itself, are made up entirely of volunteers. Members will volunteer their time and energy only if they see substantial benefit ahead. Therefore, in practice, the TC carefully works out a schedule and road map of proposed activities well in advance, giving members adequate notice to select the most relevant TFs to join and to schedule their resources to participate. Putting together a viable TF and keeping it going are no mean feats. Each member in the TC is acting on behalf of the company that volunteered his or her services to the OMG. No one is in the direct employ of the OMG, so they can't be coerced into attending meetings or threatened with replacement if they don't seem to be working out. It is also not unusual for sponsor-company duties to preempt OMG activities. Finally, many TF members often also participate in other TFs, SIGs, or OMG activities, potentially causing scheduling or workload conflicts.

Keeping everybody in the TF marching in the same direction at an even tempo is the sometimes thankless job of the TF chairman (TFC), another volunteer. The TFC organizes and conducts the meetings, ensures that minutes are taken (and distributed electronically through the TC), presents findings and recommendations to the TC, and coordinates activities with chair-persons of other TFs and the TC itself.

For Your Information

Once a new Task Force is constituted, it typically begins by refining its charter and developing a proposed schedule of activities. After that, assuming it is starting largely from scratch in a new subject area, the new TF develops a comprehensive Request For Information (RFI). Officially, the RFI is nothing more than what its name implies—a request from the TF to the industry at large to provide the OMG with any information that might be relevant to the subject area under examination. Behind its simple facade, however, each RFI serves a number of other important purposes.

First, the TF drafts the RFI. Technically speaking, a TF could simply send out a notice that said something like "Hello out there. We're a Task Force for the OMG. Please tell us everything you know about our latest hot topic, X." In practice, however, the process of drafting the RFI can be time-consuming and even controversial. Controversial? You bet. The more detailed and specific the RFI, the more likely that the responses will be truly useful to the TF's evaluation and adoption goals. To generate really useful responses, each TF must spend a lot of time up front carefully defining the topic at hand and specifying exactly what kind of information it wants to know. Otherwise, it's likely to be buried under a ton of responses that have a completely different idea from the TF of what X is, how to describe it, and why the world should be interested in it.

For this reason, a good chunk of a typical RFI ends up being cast as a kind of extension to the Object Management Architecture (OMA). It must carefully describe the purpose and scope of the technology under study, precisely define all the relevant terminology used to describe it, and provide a basic architecture that details where this technology fits into other technology areas that the OMG has completed or is considering as adoption activities.

Now, this may sound like a kind of paradox. After all, how can the TF know what to ask for until it knows what's out there? Here is where the TC's volunteer system really shines. Because the TF is already made up of OMG representatives with precisely the interests under consideration, it already has a pretty good inside track about what is likely to be submitted. In fact, the companies sending representatives to the Task Force are some of the most likely respondents to the RFI and to the later RFPs. The RFI drafting process gives them all a chance to get all of their terms, concepts, biases, and so on out in the open, and resolve them with their peers from other companies into the RFI document long before any real technology has to be submitted.

As a result, the RFI drafting process can go on for months while the TF participants haggle over terms and scope. The good news is that, by the time the RFI goes out, many of the likely respondents have already agreed on exactly what the technology is that they will be evaluating, how to describe it, and how they should be examining it. These are issues that might take years to resolve in the open marketplace—if, indeed, resolution was ever achieved at all.

By the time the RFI hits the streets, the OMG can expect to get a lot of good responses couched in exactly the terms laid down in the RFI. The typical RFI response is a statement of the respondent's current work in the TF's subject area, mapped to the terms defined in the RFI. In many cases, the respondent may already have a product that addresses that area, which can add substantially to the information that they are ready to share. Of course, RFI responses also come from companies not currently on the TF, and sometimes not even in the OMG itself—the OMG announces RFIs broadly and supplies them to just about anyone who asks. Some companies see the RFI and decide that it's high time they joined the OMG, and maybe the TF in question as well—or at least begin monitoring its activities a little closer. When outside companies do respond directly to an RFI, their responses broaden the knowledge base already available within the OMG—all of which provides additional support and publicity for the OMG and its activities.

TF members or not, many respondents to an RFI have not publicized their plans in this technology area before. Or, if they have, they described their plans using *homegrown* terminology and concepts that they invented themselves, rather than the ones agreed to in the TF for the RFI. In these cases, their response to the RFI is a kind of coming-out party, where, perhaps for the first time, they trot their new technology out to a wider audience so that it can be compared, apples to apples, with that of other companies.

Respondents to the RFI aren't required to follow all of its guidelines exactly. They can suggest new areas, terms, and formats not previously considered by the TF. Also, RFI responses needn't be from potential submitters or even vendors. Anyone with information or ideas in the RFI's subject area is invited to respond. These RFI responses serve as yet another point of input for the TF, further broadening its point of view.

By the time the RFI responses have poured in, just about everyone in the OMG who is interested in the TF's subject area now has access to a definitive collection of material indicating what many other companies are doing in this area. Moreover, the concepts are now couched in similar terminology—a great service to the object and computing communities in and of itself.

And Just What Are You Proposing?

As the TF goes through all the RFI responses, it further analyzes and organizes the information within them to prepare itself for the next step in the process: drafting the Request For Proposal (RFP). Each RFP, when complete, boils down everything that was learned from the various RFI responses into a concrete request for technology specifications to be considered for OMG adoption.

Drafting an RFP is far more grueling and time-consuming than drafting the related RFI. From the RFI responses, the members of the TF already have extracted a reasonably good idea of what's likely to be proposed by various vendors. Also, many TF members are likely to belong to companies that responded to the RFP. Therefore, many competitive pressures may be brought to bear when it comes time to define the scope and details of the RFP. For example, Company A may favor a broadly based RFP because it has a lot of working technology right now in what it defines as the TF's subject area. Company B might prefer to see a narrower scope in the first RFP, because currently it doesn't have the resources available to prepare a broader proposal, or it simply isn't that interested in the wider subject area. Company C could agree with Company A on having a broad scope, but wish to define that scope somewhat differently.

Of course, potential RFP responders are not the only organizations that might voice strong opinions on such issues as scope or detail. TF members representing the potential users of the technology under consideration often have their own ax to grind as well. For example, Company D, a user, may favor a certain approach that it has already used to create a majority of its mission-critical software. A standard that supports their existing bias would validate its decision and provide a large number of compatible suppliers in the future.

At the RFI level, where no real decisions are being made, these differences of opinion and agenda are merely placed on the table. Later, at the RFP level, both the content and wording of the proposal may have a serious effect on what can be proposed. Therefore, many issues that were loosely defined for purposes of the RFI must be tightened for the RFP, often after heated debate. And, in some cases, the TF may need to generate several different RFPs from the information gleaned from a single RFI, since a single RFP for the whole technology area would be far too broad to gain any consensus.

All this takes place under the heightened scrutiny of the rest of the OMG and the industry at large. The issuance of an RFP is viewed both within the OMG and the object computing industry at large as a major event, heralding new (or renewed) interest in the technology area at hand. Many people who have taken only a passing interest in an RFI stand up and take notice when the related RFPs are generated. Potential submitters who may have tested the water with their RFI responses (or chose to play their cards close to the vest) must also now decide if and how they present their technology for formal evaluation by the OMG.

Issuance of the RFP also sets in motion a series of events that will affect many individuals within the OMG community for some time to come. While an RFI schedule might last a few months, the evaluation and approval process for an RFP can easily extend a year or more, and will ultimately include the entire TC and the BOD. For the OMG members involved, the process of evaluating the RFP responses will be much more detailed, and involve many more people, than that required to compile the information received in response to a mere RFI.

The Moment of Truth

So, the RFP really represents a point of no return for the issuing TF and for the OMG in general. If the RFI has been thorough and the RFP is well considered and well constructed, the OMG can expect a bumper crop of appropriate responses from which to make its recommendations for the next important set of standards in object technology. If not, the entire effort could founder and a lot of people on the TF, and the OMG in general, could end up with a fair amount of egg on their faces.

Technically, however, the TC issues the RFP upon the recommendation of the TF. With this additional layer of approval required, there is no chance for a *rogue* TF to issue a faulty RFP. More important, this two-tiered approval process places the whole OMG behind the RFP. So far, this process has always yielded high-quality proposals that have garnered a solid set of responses from the vendor community. Once the RFP is issued, the most publicly visible work of the TF begins. The RFI process and the RFP drafting process both draw some outside attention, but the issuance of the RFP itself really puts things on a public footing. As the responses roll in, the official position of each of the respondents becomes solidified, and the spirited debate that marks the evaluation process begins.

The bulk of this evaluation work falls on the TF. Organizing, categorizing, and reviewing the submissions; arranging and attending submitter presentations; identifying substantive differences; obtaining clarifications; hearing recommendations from outside authorities and interest groups—all of these activities go on for months as the TF sifts through all the responses in excruciating detail. During this time, the members of the TF are under a tremendous amount of pressure. Many belong to submitter companies or to those already publicly supporting particular submitters. Yet their role in the evaluation process demands a certain amount of fairness, if not impartiality, and a need to keep close to the schedule. This will often mean compromising on some cherished points, even if they may have to face some unpleasant music from their colleagues back at company headquarters for doing so.

In the course of these evaluations, it may occur to members of the TF that much would be gained if certain submitters made changes or combined their submissions with others. According to the OMG's rules, the TF itself cannot directly request submitters to change their wording, alter their scope, merge with other submitters, or make any other such changes, even if it might vastly simplify the evaluation process. As a commercial consortium, making such suggestions might leave the OMG open to antitrust charges. However, nothing in the rules prevents the submitters, most if not all of whom are represented on the TF, from reaching these conclusions themselves. As a result, the RFP evaluation period may be punctuated with submitters amending their submissions, combining forces with other submitters behind a joint submission, or dropping out entirely.

This informal process of *natural selection* has the benefit of reducing the number of outstanding alternatives that the TF, and ultimately the TC, must formally evaluate and choose from. It also works toward building the consensus that will be necessary later to make the winning submission the de facto standard for the entire object industry.

But Will It Fly?

Eventually the list of outstanding submitters is winnowed down and the TF is ready to make an adoption recommendation to the TC. The TF is encouraged, but not compelled, to recommend a single alternative to the TC. In any case, support from the TC is crucial, since it may either vote to accept the TF's recommendation or send the TF back to generate an acceptable one. The BOD also has its say—it must formally approve the TC's adoption as being completely in the business interests of the OMG and its membership.

By now, the submitters are worn down by months of presenting, debating, revising, negotiating, and so on. Even the losers may be secretly glad when the voting is over and they can move on to other things. But the submitters of the winning proposal still have one more hurdle to cross: The OMG's adoption of their submittal is contingent on them producing a real, live commercial implementation of the endorsed specifications within six months of formal acceptance. Requiring a commercial implementation proves that the proposed specifications are not sheer fantasy. In other words, the OMG wants to eliminate all doubt as to whether the proposal they end up endorsing can actually be implemented. A very expeditious way to do this, obviously, is simply to require that such an implementation be delivered in reasonably short order in commercial-grade form.

According to the OMG's rules, a commercial implementation associated with a proposal is due only if that proposal is accepted for adoption by the OMG. Furthermore, as we just mentioned, the due date is not immediately upon adoption, but six months later. Structuring the implementation requirement in this manner cleverly gets around a number of potential problems. For example, if the OMG required an existing commercial implementation for each submission at submission time, submitters with suitable products that might be well along in the lab but not yet released strictly for commercial reasons would be kept out of the process. Instead, the OMG gives submitters at least six months, plus the time during which submissions are under evaluation. This is usually at least a full year in total, more than enough time to get the latest technology out of the lab and into the hands of the public.

Furthermore, it also gives a submitter a good deal of time to make any changes or upgrades that may be required, for example, to merge its submission with other submitters. Even if a submitter actually had a commercial implementation at submittal time, forcing them to produce it would discourage such changes and repositioning and tend to harden the positions taken during the evaluation process. Under the current requirements, submitters can easily make changes to their positions even up to the very end of the evaluation process and still have time to update their commercial implementations if they win.

On the other hand, waiting the extra six months for a commercial implementation is no real hardship for the OMG or the object computing public. In fact, it actually gives vendors other than the submitters a chance to catch up and offer their own competitive commercial versions of the winning specifications or of extensions and improvements. This translates to more support for the adoption and more options for computing consumers.

Another important benefit from the OMG's perspective is that the current scheme has the effect of allowing the marketplace to do its own de facto enforcement of its requirement for a commercial implementation. In other words, the OMG can generally count on the fact that no vendor is likely to risk the embarrassment of submitting something that, more than a year after submittal, is not yet commercially viable. This saves the OMG the time, trouble, and expense of doing its own exhaustive evaluations—something it really has too few technical resources to do. Therefore, in the end, the cost for the OMG to require a commercial implementation is practically zero, but, of course, the credibility win for all concerned is enormous. Vendors are, in effect, knocking themselves out to participate in, and bless, the OMG's technically nonbinding approval process. The winners then provide, at their own expense, real, live commercial implementations that serve to prove to prospective users that OMG-endorsed technology actually works.

This *have your cake and eat it, too* approach has helped fuel the enormous steady growth of the OMG and its rapid acceptance in the overall computer industry marketplace. The result? Although the OMG is not officially in the standards game at all, it is now the first place that people go to when they want to know about standards for object technology.

With this in mind, let's take a closer look at how the OMG's adoption process has actually worked. To do so, we'll discuss in some detail the development and release of the OMG's Common Object Request Broker Architecture (CORBA), its best-known and most widely adopted set of specifications for object technology. The CORBA was also the OMG's first adoption effort and, in many ways, set the pattern for how the OMG now operates and is likely to operate in the future.

THE STANDARD STORY

Mention the OMG to anyone in the object technology industry today, and the terms *ORB* and *CORBA* are sure to soon follow. ORB, as we've already discussed, is short for Object Request Broker, and CORBA (Common Object Request Broker Architecture) is the OMG-endorsed standard for ORBs.

The ORB, you'll recall, is at the center of the OMG's Object Management Architecture (OMA). It's the architectural component that all other components—Object Services, Common Facilities, and Application-Objects—plug into. Like a kind of object-oriented telephone switching system, it allows all these components to talk to one another by shuttling messages among them.

The basic idea was simple. Object languages provide a way to define objects and send messages among them, but only on a single machine and usually only on a single process. These languages typically provide no explicit facilities for objects to send messages to other processes or remote machines, much less to objects written in a different language and/or running on a different type of operating system or hardware platform.

But the environment that most customers desire is now often both heterogeneous and distributed over networks. Allowing objects to communicate only within a single, homogeneous process space would make each application and each platform a computing island. To be truly successful in the commercial marketplace, the object industry must offer some way to allow objects to send messages outside of traditional process boundaries. As we discussed very early on in this book, one idea is the *meganet* (the logical network of all systems in an enterprise and even across enterprises that will allow a complete integration and interoperation of all computing resources) and its new virtual machine.

In the not-so-distant future, such capabilities are likely to become commonplace. Already, a variety of tools, libraries, and even language extensions support various degrees of distributed object-messaging implicitly. In 1990, however, when the OMG began to actively consider the ORB, very little of this sort of thing existed, at least in anything resembling a commercially viable state. By proposing to recommend a standard specification in this area, the OMG appeared to be jumping well ahead of the commercial marketplace. However, the OMG's own architecture clearly shows just how key the ORB is to the entire object paradigm.

Without the ORB, the other parts of the architecture would be pretty much hanging out in space, unable to hook up to each other or to anything else.

Despite the lack of any commercially available ORB technology, the members of the OMG were aware of a number of distributed object computing environments under development that were on the road to commercialization. They reasoned that, in the year or two it would take to go through the RFI, RFP, and evaluation processes that lie ahead, many vendors would complete their products in this area and be ready to go public. In addition, it was always possible that the RFI and RFP processes might shake some hitherto unknown technology out of the trees. Since there had never been a forum like the OMG before, it was a reasonably safe bet that at least a few companies were no doubt working on technology similar to the ORB, which had not yet seen the light of day outside of their own development labs.

In short, moving forward to standardize the ORB was a risk for the OMG, but a calculated risk worth taking. Very little in the way of proven implementations might be available, but commercialization would not be required until late in the process, anyway. While the process was going on, and certainly by the time it neared completion, submitter companies would have every incentive to spruce up their products and prepare them for commercialization.

In any case, an open forum would finally get the majority of work in this area out on the table. While some companies might be reluctant to publicize their latest technology unilaterally, opening up inside an industry group, such as the OMG, where everyone else is doing pretty much the same thing, is generally a lot more comfortable. Everyone would share ideas, and this would in itself tend to promote a certain amount of standardization and interoperability over the long run.

The New Kid on the Block

The OMG Technical Committee chartered the ORB Task Force in October 1990, less than one year after the OMG itself was founded. Besides developing the OMA Guide and continuing some ongoing internal work on a high-level object model, the ORB TF represented the first major technical effort by the OMG—certainly the first aimed at endorsing commercial technology. As a result, all eyes would be on the ORB TF, not only to assess the incoming technology, but also to assess the process it would use for evaluations and overall viability of the OMG's adoption approach. Could the OMG really succeed where so many others had bogged down? Could it produce useful standards that would gain widespread acceptance?

The creation of the ORB TF certainly had at least one immediate effect on the OMG. As word got around about the importance of the ORB, the OMG's own membership began to grow rapidly. In May 1990, soon after the TF was chartered, the membership head count was 52; by March 1991, it had already reached 100. This expanded membership, which now included most major hardware and software vendors, assured that the Technical Committee and the ORB Task Force would be highly representative of the industry, and also likely to become the forum for some spirited debate. As the ORB TF carried on, membership continued to grow apace, reaching nearly 200 before the CORBA specification was finally endorsed.

As the membership expanded and the work of the Task Force progressed, the tone and tenor of TC and TF meetings began to change perceptibly. At first, the bulk of the work was done by a few stalwarts from the founding members, who knew each other so well that meetings sometimes had the feeling of a small, exclusive club. But, as the new members got acclimated, they gradually worked themselves into the routine, greatly expanding the range of ideas and personality styles that served as input to the whole process. As submitters responded to the Request For Information (RFI) and then the Request For Proposal (RFP), it became clear that the range of different ideas about objects was much greater than anyone expected. Prior to this process, most delegates were familiar with objects only in terms of what they and their coworkers had been working on internally, often in great secrecy. Suddenly they discovered that many other people were working on the same problem, and not necessarily reaching the same conclusions.

Sometimes the experiential gap among the various submitters (and among the evaluators) was so wide that it was often hard to believe that they were really talking about the same RFP. In many cases, members used widely different terms to mean the same thing, the same terms to mean widely different things, and placed significantly different weights on the relative importance of the various architectural components of the submissions. Because the process was so new, a number of problems surfaced that no one was particularly prepared for. First, a number of RFP submitters had never answered the RFI, so the RFP had never really reflected their information or point of view. In addition, some RFI submitters radically changed what they later submitted in response to the RFP.

It became clear that both the technology under review and the TF process itself were so formative that the viewpoints of submitters and evaluators alike continued changing radically even after the RFP responses were in hand. After seeing the other submissions and getting back some response to their own, a number of submitters requested, and were granted, the opportunity to resubmit an amended response to the RFP. Some of these amended responses again introduced substantially different material.

The Grand Alliance

All this hubbub began to take a toll on the submitters *and* the evaluators. Both were climbing an enormous learning curve, trying to keep up with the changing submissions, and trying to understand, compare, and reconcile what were often widely differing points of view. As a result, the evaluation process dragged on somewhat longer than expected, and individual patience was often stretched to the limit. At the same time, something wonderful was happening. As the evaluators hacked their way through the mounds of submissions, a kind of unofficial consensus was beginning to emerge within the group. After months of discussion, they had developed a common terminology—even if they didn't always agree, at least they could understand and communicate with each other.

Furthermore, after pondering the many ideas raised in proposals and discussions, most of the TF members had softened and broadened their original points of view. They began to integrate all of these new ideas in their minds, and realized that the total picture was much larger than any had imagined on their own. As a result, it became progressively clearer to most of the ORB TF that, while almost all of the submissions clearly had substantial merit, none of them was really complete enough by itself to become a standard. The idea began to emerge that the only acceptable result would be some kind of compromise or merger that included important elements from each of several leading proposals.

Of course, the OMG's rules do not allow it to officially suggest such a compromise or merger—an antitrust no-no. But those same rules are flexible enough to allow submitters to reach such conclusions on their own and amend their positions and proposals accordingly. Just such a process had actually begun early in the evaluation cycle. Leading submitters realized they had much in common and more to gain by combining forces than by butting heads. At the same time, other submitters (who had gained only marginal support for their own proposals) realized that their best bet was to back one of the leaders closest to their point of view. Since nobody yet had an established market position, this decision was a relatively painless one to make.

From an original field of almost a dozen proposals, therefore, two main merged submissions eventually emerged: One was led by Sun and HP, which had officially merged their own proposals and had even announced a joint agreement to develop and commercialize the technology it was based on. The second camp was led by DEC and Hyperdesk, a spin-off from Data General. NCR, which had led a strong third camp through most of the evaluation process, ultimately decided to withdraw its independent proposal and endorse the Sun/HP submission.

This natural process of convergence greatly simplified the evaluation problem immediately facing the ORB TF and also indicated that the OMG's approach was heading in the right direction. In effect, the OMG was acting as a catalyst to normal market forces, a forum for shaking out the key issues that would face vendors and users alike, well before any major commercial commitments had been made. If nothing else, this process created a commonly accepted terminology and frame of reference for describing object technology early in its life cycle, eliminating many years of marketplace confusion that has usually accompanied the commercial introduction of a new technology. Through the OMG, the entire object industry was already speaking a common language, even though not everyone agreed exactly on the content of the message being communicated.

Many Voices, a Single ORB

Having successfully winnowed the field down to just two submissions, the ORB Task Force began the process of exhaustively comparing the two submissions in order to make a final recommendation to the OMG's Technical Committee. Although the TF evaluation process had already leveled much of the playing field in respect to terminology, the two submissions could otherwise hardly have been more different.

A full discussion of the differences between the two submissions is certainly beyond the scope of this book, and mostly of academic interest now, anyway. The important point is that, as the evaluation process moved along, most of the TF came to this conclusion: *Both* proposals had elements that, if properly combined, would appeal to a far broader audience than either proposal by itself. Rather than a winner and a loser, the majority of the TF, and the TC, wanted to see two collaborating winners. The mood of the TF and TC was not lost on the two submission groups. As the date for the TC's final recommendation vote grew near, the two met jointly and agreed to ask the TF for a 90-day period in which to organize their separate submissions into a single, unified one. Both realized that unanimous acceptance of a single proposal was the best possible outcome for everyone.

As hoped, the OMG's flexible process worked to lubricate natural market forces. Eventually the industry would have to agree on a single standard for distributed object messaging—a common ORB—or face self-defeating fragmentation. Without the OMG, this issue might have taken years or even decades to sort out. Instead, without issuing any edicts or forcing anyone's hand, the OMG generated a wide consensus of vendors and users about the basic specifications of distributed object environments before any products were out the door.

For better or worse, the CORBA specification now epitomizes the mainstream view of commercial ORBs and distributed object computing environments for the foreseeable future. After all those months of evaluation, debate, and compromise by the object industry's best technical minds, the CORBA reflects a technical environment we can all live with for a while. Let's take a closer look at CORBA and see just what kind of object request broker the OMG and its members finally got for all their time and trouble.

CORBA, CORBA

The basic notion behind CORBA is to provide a uniform way for any object to receive and respond to a request from any requester (*client*), either another object or even a traditional nonobject-oriented program. Once such a request is made, the ORB makes sure that the request is delivered to an appropriate receiving object, no matter where it is and how it is implemented. If the object generates a request while processing the request, the ORB must deliver that request back to the client.

As indicated earlier, one of the main purposes of an ORB is to relieve the client and the receiving objects from keeping up with all the details involved in actually delivering requests. In fact, the sender and receiver of a given request need to know only one thing about each other to send and process that request: the interface required to formulate the request. In this respect, the ORB truly acts as a broker, much like a stockbroker or real estate broker. After all, a stockbroker is not just some guy or gal in a business suit who constantly tries to sell us securities to maximize commissions—although this sometimes appears to be their function. In reality, the broker is first and foremost an intermediary between us and the market—in this case, millions of others who have stocks to buy or sell.

If you decide to buy some shares of stock, you must somehow locate someone who wants to sell their shares of the same stock. If there were no brokers, you would have to somehow advertise your desire to buy the stock, hope someone in a selling mood would respond, and then negotiate with everybody who did. To complete the transaction, you would end up knowing quite a lot about the seller (and vice versa) that is not really relevant to your mutual desire to transfer some stock. However, since we all must work through a broker, we don't have to worry about who the seller might be. It could be a giant mutual fund in New York City, a government pension fund in California, a senior citizen in Des Moines,

Broker—The Intermediary Between Buyers and Sellers.

or, for a large enough order, all of them combined. Due to the miracle of the stock market and the brokers who run it, you don't have to know who the other buyers and sellers are, and they don't have to know who you are.

This *brokering* concept works even if the product being brokered is a more unique a commodity than stocks, bonds, or pork bellies. For example, if you want to buy a particular piece of real estate that is listed by a broker, you can, in theory, complete all negotiations and transactions without ever dealing with the owner or owners. The broker acts as the intermediary and handles all the details.

Within the world of objects, an ORB works pretty much the same way. At one end, objects that can handle requests register with the ORB, saying they are available. At the other end, clients make requests for the objects that are available. The broker makes sure that the client's requests are delivered to the appropriate objects regardless of the effort required. For example, let's say that we want to create a personal loan application-processing system. After we have input the customer's personal data, we want to access a *credit analysis*-object to determine credit worthiness. Let's assume that we know how to make such a request but have no idea where the credit analysis-object lives or how it is implemented.

However, we do know how to contact an appropriate broker—in this case, the Object Request Broker (ORB). We place our request for a credit analysis to the ORB, which is responsible for making sure our request is delivered to the appropriate object. The broker knows about that object and where it is located, because the object registered itself with the ORB sometime before. After the object processes the request, its response—in this case, *qualified* or *unqualified*—is returned through the ORB to the client-object that requested it. Our loan-application system works. Thanks to the ORB, a client-object and a credit analysis-object have successfully interacted without knowing anything much about each other.

Anyone familiar with traditional information systems knows well that what we have described is certainly a different way of thinking about accessing one program from another than what has come before. Traditionally, if our loan-application system wanted to obtain a credit analysis, it would have to know exactly where the credit analysis program was located, what communications protocol was necessary to connect to it, and probably what language it was implemented in so that we could properly formulate the request.

Not only was such a traditional application a *lot* of trouble to implement, but it also could fall apart if anyone made the slightest change to any part of the system. For example, what if we moved the credit analysis program to a different machine, or changed the networking protocols available on its processor? In either case, we would have to hunt down every requester of the credit analysis program and make the necessary changes within them to be able to continue accessing the credit analysis program.

An ORB does away with all this toil and trouble for all time. By brokering every request, the ORB makes sure that clients never need to know anything ever again about where objects are located, or how they are implemented. Clients just make their requests in a standard form to the ORB and—*voilà*—the requests are delivered. Never will we have to *reimplement* a client just to access an outside object or program, no matter how much its implementation might change. The ORB must work its tail off to accomplish its automagical mission. It must register objects, accept requests, successfully deliver those requests, and return the resultant responses. In addition, it must perform a number of housekeeping functions: error checking, exception handling, and so on. Having the ORB handle this for us, however, is a whole lot better than placing the burden on each client and object.

All of this would be of limited value if the ORB were not completely standardized. Even a weak OMG standard would probably ensure that each ORB contained a standard way to register objects and make requests, and this would be great. *But*, when it came time to install a new ORB or to try to access an object on a different ORB, we'd be almost back to square one. For each client and object, there would have to be a different implementation for each ORB that they might run on, and no standard way to access across ORBs at all.

This is where CORBA comes in. The basic idea is to have the CORBA specify enough of the interfaces for all ORBs so that they can work and play happily together. This includes a guarantee that they can all accept the same clients and objects without modification, and that they can all exchange requests transparently. At this writing, not all the necessary pieces are yet in place for this to happen, but CORBA is already making giant strides in this direction. In addition, the OMG is pledged to keep improving CORBA until it meets this goal.

Now, all CORBA-compliant ORBs will not be exactly the same. In fact, each ORB could be implemented completely differently to emphasize different features but still meet the CORBA specifications. For example, some ORBs could be implemented to maximize the speed of individual request handling, others to handle heavy request volumes without slowing down, others to simplify installation and configuration, and so on. None of these implementation-dependent features is likely to ever fall within the scope of the specifications.

However, no matter how it was implemented, each CORBA-compliant ORB would maintain, as a subset of its own interface, a set of interface elements specifically designed to interoperate with other compliant ORBs and handle all clients and servers. If we want to be clever about it, we could even think of any compliant ORB as an object itself, a member of the *CORBA* class (or one of its subclasses), guaranteed to have the CORBA interface specified by the OMG, and thus be compatible and interoperable with every other member of the *CORBA* class.

IDL Chatter

Another way to look at ORBs is to think of each ORB in the same way that you think of the message-deliverer that comes automatically with every object language. Each message-deliverer provides a standard mechanism for objects to make and respond to requests within that object language. The main difference between ORBs and message-deliverers is that an object language message-deliverer handles requests only among objects written in that language and running in the same process space. An ORB, on the other hand, happily crosses language and process-space boundaries to deliver its requests.

However, in order to do this, the ORB itself must have some kind of language to be able to handle requests and describe the interfaces of the objects that generate those requests. The CORBA standard for such a language is called the Interface Definition Language (IDL), which is a little like Esperanto (the *universal language* that was supposed to break down language barriers among people a few decades back). The big difference here is that the IDL works! In fact, it is such a vital part of the CORBA standard that its precise definition takes up a hefty percentage of the overall specifications.

There is nothing particularly exciting or unique about the CORBA IDL. In fact, it looks a lot like C++, or at least the part of C++ that defines classes, with some extensions to handle distributed messaging. However, unlike C++ or COBOL—or any other previous computer language, for that matter—it does not contain any grammar or syntax for executing logic. As a result, it is impossible to write a regular computer program in IDL. But, then again, no one should ever need to do so; they need only to implement their objects in any language they like and then describe the interface for each class of object in IDL. Once this is done, the ORB can accept requests from any client and deliver them to the appropriate receivers.

Now, the nifty thing about every ORB that complies with the CORBA specification is that all CORBA ORBs can understand IDL. If you've successfully implemented an object class in IDL-speak and described its interface in IDL-speak, all within one system, you are free to move any object of that class to any other CORBA-compliant ORB and the object will fit in just fine with all the other objects. So, by defining a standard IDL, CORBA has taken a giant step toward the goal of significant object interoperability.

Skeletons, Stubs, and Other Strange Creatures

Now that you understand the primary role of the IDL, there's just a bit more you need to understand about how it works with clients, objects, requests, and the ORB. This discussion is a bit more technical than anything we've covered so far, but it's worth it if it gives you a better grasp of the CORBA specifications.

Let's assume that you've created an object class and described its interface in IDL. Now the questions are: How does an object of this class actually hook itself into the ORB, and how does a client making a request to that object hook *itself* into the ORB? The basic answer is that the IDL for that object is run through a special IDL compiler, the results of which are used to bind both the clients and the objects to the ORB. Basically, the IDL compiler generates what are called *skeletons* and *stubs*. Skeletons are the way the ORB actually calls objects accessed, while stubs are the way that clients actually call the ORB with their requests. If this all sounds a little strange, please bear with me.

Just imagine now that you have run your IDL compiler and generated one skeleton and one stub for each IDL definition. On the client side, you install a stub that basically looks like a local version of the object being called. However, when the client sends a request to the stub, the stub translates the request into a direct call to the ORB. The ORB then does whatever internal magic is necessary to locate the object being accessed and delivers the request to the skeleton. Finally, the skeleton makes the actual method call to the object specified in the request.

Each different implementation of a CORBA-compliant ORB will have its own IDL compiler and will generate appropriate stubs and skeletons that hook to that implementation. There may also be different stubs and skeletons generated, depending on the languages used to implement the objects and clients. However, all this is basically academic to most ORB users. According to CORBA, no matter how it is compiled, the only object-specification language users will really have to know is IDL. CORBA does define a few additional areas that might be of interest to some users. For example, it defines *dynamic invocation*, a way for clients to construct requests *on the fly* without going through stubs. It also has a similar concept—*object adapters*—that can replace skeletons. CORBA even defines the notion of *language mapping*, a concept that allows clients to make requests through the syntax of their own programming language without being directly aware of either stubs or dynamic invocation.

All of these extra components and features are largely designed to give vendors and users a number of ways to extend or customize their ORBs while remaining CORBA compliant. As some of these features become better known and used, you can expect future revisions of CORBA, revisions that better standardize how ORBs work and interface to clients, objects, and one another.

Making CORBA Work

Even the mile-high flyby of the OMG's CORBA you just received has revealed that this set of standards specifications is extensive and, in some parts, quite detailed. At the same time, CORBA leaves a lot of loose ends that will have to be tied up over time. This work will be done either piecemeal by ORB implementors and users, or by an ongoing effort to extend and revise the CORBA standard as the market and technology mature.

The OMG is not unaware of this need for an evolution of the CORBA standard, and already has plans for revisions 2 and 3 in the works. The schedule for these planned versions will last at least until 1995. By then, CORBA will be pushing its half-decade mark and, it is hoped, will be widely accepted and implemented across the industry. However, for the OMG's CORBA to be truly usable as an industry standard for a wide range of commercial applications, much more work needs to done. No matter how good the CORBA specification becomes, it still focuses primarily on the mechanism that delivers requests to objects. No one could build a large-scale distributed object environment based on CORBA alone.

At a minimum, commercial CORBA implementations will need to be supported by a comprehensive set of object services providing such key features as security, storage, transaction control, versioning, archiving, exception handling, and so on. Fortunately, the CORBA IDL now gives us a way of specifying the interfaces to such services in a consistent manner, but CORBA itself is silent on what supporting services are required, or what their interfaces would look like.

It is no surprise, therefore, that the OMG's most active Task Force since the completion of the first version of CORBA has been the Object Services Task Force (OSTF). Between its founding in 1992 and late in 1995, the OSTF will be very busy going through a series of RFIs and RFPs covering a comprehensive set of object services. Many of these services are highly interdependent (for example, versioning depends on storage), so this should be a very large and difficult effort, and quite interesting to watch.

Something else that commercial CORBA implementations will certainly need is better and more standard sets of software tools. Although CORBA postulates the existence of an IDL compiler, the current CORBA doesn't specify anything about how this tool will work, or anything at all about any other tools. At a bare minimum, we know that we will need tools to install and configure the ORB, to install new objects and interfaces, to keep track of available stubs, skeletons, and adapters, and so on. In addition, such tools need to be specified so that they themselves interoperate and share information, even across multiple ORBs. In this area, the OMG is likely to collaborate with existing efforts to standardize interoperability among all development tools, such as the European-initiated Portable Common Tools Environment (PCTE).

CORBA will also become more important if and when the OMG is able to endorse standard specifications for Common Facilities. The OMG intends to make sure that such popular facilities as electronic mail, database access, help facilities, and compound document editors—to name a few—are all eventually standardized around CORBA IDL specifications. This will add a lot more muscle to the OMG's story that CORBA should become the backbone specification for mainstream business computing environments. So, with as much as the OMG has already accomplished in its relatively short existence, and with as much credibility and momentum that it has generated in the industry at large, its battle to set standards for objects and distributed computing environments is really just beginning.

In the next chapter, I'll haul out my personal crystal ball and try to guess what will be happening over the next decade or so in terms of object technology in the business computing world. I'll also give a bit of thought to an all-important issue: how companies like yours can best migrate to object computing as the technology matures and gains broader acceptance.

CHAPTER 7

Objects in Your Future

GAZING INTO THE CRYSTAL OBJECT

In the first part of this book, I developed a rationale for explaining why object technology is a natural fit for the next generation of business computing systems. I described how object technology readily supports change (the common denominator of all modern business) and how it supports important business trends towards decentralization, globalization, and so on. I indicated that objects are that all-important modular component, the software building block of virtually every industry, and indeed of business itself.

"So," you might be tempted to ask, "does all this mean that objects are inevitable? Is object technology so logical, so intuitive, and so compelling that everyone who is anyone in business computing will buy wholeheartedly into the object paradigm? That businesses will begin migrating their systems and organizations accordingly? Are we all about to wake up one morning and find ourselves squarely positioned in a new era—the *Golden Age of Objects*? Are those objects in my rearview mirror closer than they appear?"

On the surface, the answer to these questions would appear to be a firm *yes*. The intuitive benefits of object technology are now rapidly propelling it out of the development skunk works and into the mainstream information systems process. This steadily rising interest in objects has, for example, propelled the OMG to become the single largest trade organization in the computer industry. Meanwhile, vendors and users alike have fallen all over each other announcing major, new object-oriented initiatives, and overall spending on object-oriented development is growing at a feverish pace.

145

It's a safe bet that everyone in the business computing world will be encountering objects and object technology in some form or other over the next few years. Soon mainstream IT professionals will begin talking about objects in the same way that they used to talk about PCs, databases, GUIs, networks, and all those other *new* technologies of the last decade. If this indeed happens, it will certainly make those of us who have invested time, money, and energy in the object industry very happy. Vendors of object-oriented development products, such as languages and databases, will sell a lot more product, and object-oriented consultants will get larger—and more lucrative—assignments. At the same time, any corporate information systems professionals prescient enough to have backed objects will get a definite career boost.

For those with a limited idea of what object technology can potentially provide, this first-round financial success will be more than enough reward. Just as others did earlier with databases, GUIs, and networks, garden-variety object technologists will prosper comfortably by carving out a niche for objects within the computing industry as a whole. However, those with a broader vision for objects will find that financial success alone is a substantial disappointment. Why? Because object visionaries see object technology as more than just a better way to build the same types of computing applications, and more than just another layer on top of other software technologies. They see object technology as the foundation for a whole new way of doing supporting business: rapidly creating new solutions from leverageable, reusable business computing components while integrating diverse and complex networks of computing resources.

Now, in one sense, I could probably argue that this sort of vision is also inevitable. Eventually, competitive pressures will drive some companies to seek fundamental changes in the way in which they develop, support, and utilize information systems. At that point, I feel comfortable in predicting that some form of component software technology—regardless of whether it is called *objects*—will be a large part of that change. But, will these changes happen over the next 5 to 15 years, or 50 to 100 years? In the grand scheme of history, of course, that's not a significant question. As a futurist, I can be fairly confident of my main conclusions: Objects will eventually prevail, there will be a worldwide meganet, businesses will soon mutate and coordinate their information systems on demand, and so on. Whether this happens next week, next year, next century, or next generation is not a pressing concern to those of us fortunate enough to indulge in pure futurism.

But contemporary mortals trying to survive in today's complex, ever-changing business computing jungle have a legitimate interest in just how long this object revolution will really take. When you think about objects from this perspective, you want to know where you stand. Are you a Leonardo da Vinci, a visionary hoping that man might one day soar aloft on mechanical flapping wings, or a modern-day Wright brother, witness and catalyst to the founding of a worldwide transportation system that will grow from infancy to maturity in a single human generation?

Those Teeming Masses, Yearning to Have Objects

This is precisely the question that many information systems professionals are beginning to think about today. Not long ago, the OMG commissioned an in-depth study to find out exactly what ordinary IS mortals think about the future of object technology. The results show just how much this new technology has already penetrated the collective psyche of the business computing mainstream.

The study, conducted by a well-known survey research company, included a representative sampling of about 250 information systems directors, application development managers, end-user managers, and data communication managers. Also interviewed were a number of industry experts, whose views were compared in the study report to those of the working professionals. First of all, the response rate to this study was over 80 percent, a fact that is itself indicative of the interest that object technology is generating in every corner of the industry. In addition, the working professionals were actually more positive and enthusiastic than the experts about the likely rate of adoption for object technology. They actually complained that vendors were not supplying solutions fast enough to suit their perceived need for immediate object-based technology solutions. More specifically, the study asked these professionals to rank four possible scenarios about the future of object technology. The scenarios ranked from highly optimistic to very pessimistic, so there was one suited to almost any opinion.

The most gloomy scenario—I'll call it *More of the Same*—paints the picture that object technology is basically a lot of hype and will soon collapse under its own dead and useless weight. According to this view, vendors will completely fail to deliver usable application development tools for objects, and similarly fail to deliver a viable infrastructure to connect object systems and applications enterprise-wide.

The next scenario—let's call it *Embedded OT*—is a bit more positive but very limiting. It suggests that object technology will become the backbone of many if not most vendor products, but have only an indirect impact on end-user business applications development. In other words, more familiar tools such as databases, operating systems, and packaged applications will increasingly be built using object technology inside, but end-user developers will continue to use traditional tools and methodologies, and not really become directly involved in OT.

Moving on up, the next scenario—*OT As Methodology*—contends that object technology will become a leading-edge approach to building end-user applications in terms of programming languages, databases, operating systems, and other development tools. These tools will be marketed as object-oriented, a moniker that will be associated with more rapid development, less maintenance, and lower development costs. However, in this scenario, there is little or no notion of a market for objects themselves—just for the tools and methodologies for corporate developers to build them on a custom basis.

The last and most optimistic scenario—*Next Generation*—suggests that object technology will become the basis for a whole new approach to business computing systems and their development. In this view, developers will actually purchase commercially developed objects from a range of software vendors and use them to assemble new applications. Business-level as well as system-level objects will be available, with many targeted directly to end users as opposed to information systems professionals.

So, what did the hardworking mainstream information systems professionals have to say about these scenarios? Well, first of all, they largely rejected out of hand the two most pessimistic scenarios—*More of the Same* and *Embedded OT*. Only a paltry 20 percent thought either scenario was very likely. Of the two remaining scenarios—*OT As Methodology* and *Next Generation*—each garnered more than twice the support of the most pessimistic scenarios. *OT As Methodology* was the dominant choice—about half—but about 40 percent also thought *Next Generation* was either likely or extremely likely.

Lead or Get Out of the Way

All of this is amazing, especially considering that any mainstream commercial awareness of object technology is a brand-new phenomenon. In just five or six years from its serious introduction into the marketplace, and with only a tiny percentage of the actual dollar market for computing products and services, object technology is already here to stay in a substantial way.

Digging a little deeper into the study, you'll find something else of interest: The professionals who expressed reservations about object technology tended not to fault the technology itself. Instead, they cited various industry factors—specifically, a lack of standards and commercially available infrastructures to tie objects and object systems together—as reasons for their concern. Mostly, though, they thought objects were the way to go, but doubted that anyone—vendors or users—would be able to adapt rapidly enough to supply real object applications and tools anytime soon. In other words, the study clearly shows that, given the opportunity and the proper support from the computer-vendor community, most information systems professionals will gladly move to objects as fast as they can. Fully one quarter, for example, believe that object technology will be pervasive by 1996. Regardless of whether this actually happens, rapid migration to objects is high in the minds of a substantial group of industry professionals.

Interestingly enough, one of the most common concerns cited in the report about the future of object technology relates to the job that computer industry vendors are doing in terms of preparing users for this new technology. The single most common complaint of both experts and end-user professionals alike was that vendors are doing an exceedingly poor job in the positioning of the technology to users, and in providing them with the training they need to evaluate and assess its potential. In their view, this lack of in-depth vendor support is seriously holding up the wider adoption of object technology and may be seriously jeopardizing its future.

Unfortunately, this is one of those conclusions that must be true because people think it is. By definition, if experts and end users alike feel that vendors are holding up the works in respect to object technology, it must be so. Of course, this begs the next question: Why would vendors hold up the adoption of object technology? Why aren't they wholeheartedly leading their customers into this promising new technology?

The main reason why vendors may appear to be lagging behind user demand in the area of object technology is actually pretty simple—vendors make money only by selling what they have, and most vendors are still just getting their object technology product strategy in order. It will take most vendor organizations at least a few years, if not longer, to decide which object products and services to build, which to acquire, how to integrate them, how to package and price them, how to position them in respect to their traditional product lines, and so on. A significant *shakeout* period is necessary before the vendor community can be expected to bring object technology into its bread-and-butter accounts. This shakeout will take place within each vendor organization and across the vendor community at large. Some vendors will bet the farm on objects, but others will hold back until they feel that their own organizations, and the market in general, is ready for a wholesale transition to this new technology.

This more conservative strategy is understandable, and would probably be acceptable under normal circumstances. After all, vendors and users can both point to a variety of novel technologies—relational database, AI, structured programming, and CASE, just to name a few—that promised to take the world by storm and ended up costing everyone a lot of money and sleep in exchange for less-than-overwhelming benefits. Why shouldn't the vendor community be more than a little cautious about object technology as well?

Unfortunately, vendors who take this conventional approach are very likely to be disappointed again, but for the opposite reasons—they are very likely to get blindsided by the coming tidal wave of user interest in objects. In the process, they may lose the initiative in the object revolution—and their market position—in the process. Such vendors should take the study that I just cited as at least one *early warning* of what is just over the horizon, and strongly reconsider their object strategy. They may find that, if they don't lead, they may be forced out of the way. And, by the way, much the same warning could be made for users who insist on sitting on the object fence too long.

The Ubiquitous Object

Why is this so? What makes objects so different from the many other upstart technologies that have disappointed the marketplace in the past? The reason is a direct outgrowth of what I have already discussed throughout this book—that objects are really just the flip side of the component revolution we have already experienced in hardware. They are the software equivalent of the microchip and its ubiquitous progeny, the personal computer.

As we all well know, the microchip and the PC were the growth hormones that transformed Intel, Apple, and Microsoft from midgets to giants—and new household words—in less than a decade. And who can forget that a large chunk of each company's good fortune was carved from the hides of their traditional competitors, many of whom are now being unkindly compared to the dinosaurs of old? What if the next fortunes to be made and lost are in the object business? A number of facts suggest that this might be the case. If we look at the phenomenon of the microchip, we see that its success is rooted in its universality. The microchip is such a fundamental building block of hardware technology that it is as likely to make its appearance in a toaster oven or microwave as in a fancy desktop computer. In fact, Intel and its fellow microchip producers were able to make their very first fortunes servicing such unglamorous markets, and many still do well continuing to service them today. In this respect, the resemblance of the object to the microchip is almost uncanny. Like microchips, objects are likely to turn up in virtually any type of application, from printer drivers to accounting systems, from workgroup software to data acquisition services. They can be used to create single-user personal productivity packages or to manage globally distributed computing environments.

Even as the commercial object industry barely starts to dry behind the ears, objects are already predominant in such system software areas as graphical user interfaces, network management software, and operating system components. Even more important, objects are starting to crop up in a wide range of business domains, and not just as implementation tools. Developers are beginning to discover that no application domain is so large—or so small—that the object paradigm cannot be profitably applied to model it, even when something other than an object language may be used to actually implement it. Even otherwise conservative software organizations are strongly considering turning to objects as an architectural and design paradigm, even if they've yet to write a single line of object-oriented code.

What is interesting about this phenomenon is that it doesn't take any special tools or techniques to use objects in this way. Of course, better tools would be welcome, but it's very possible to put together a useful object-oriented design, and to even write a significant object-oriented application, if only by applying some bubble gum and baling wire to what's already on the market today.

IBM was instrumental in popularizing the PC, but the first big success story in this area was Apple. We shouldn't forget that it was possible for Jobs and Wozniak to create the first Apple personal computer in their garage out of assorted microprocessor parts bought at a secondhand electronics store. In much the same way, upstart vendors and users are beginning to design and construct object-oriented applications and services from whatever object tools are currently available. The results aren't necessarily elegant but, for the most part, they have been worth the effort. Of course, these early successes, no matter how modest, simply act to drive the demand for more and better object design and construction tools, and eventually for *finished* reusable objects themselves.

If the big vendors aren't quite ready to deliver a total set of object solutions just yet, that's unlikely to discourage those that have already caught the object bug. They'll be more than willing to experiment with the new tools brought out early by upstart cottage object vendors, or *roll their own* tools and techniques. This is, of course, exactly the type of dynamic that drove the proliferation of the PC. Users bought PCs and PC software in droves regardless of whether the major vendors had anything to offer. Upstart vendors with any PCs at all to sell, or any software to run on them, made fortunes, as the major vendors struggled to come to grips with this new reality and position themselves accordingly. Some never made it at all.

Within traditional information systems organizations, the same drama was played out in microcosm. Users bought PCs and PC software, regardless of whether IS sanctioned them. If the IS group did offer leadership in the PC area, users generally took it. But, if nothing of the sort was forthcoming, these users simply went outside for products and services, or somehow managed to roll their own.

Similar scenarios are already starting to play themselves out in the object business. A taste for objects is invading both the user and developer communities much faster than established vendors or traditional information systems organizations can hope to control it. Within a few years, objects will have become as ubiquitous as the microchips and PCs they run on. Moreover, only those vendors with coherent and compelling object strategies will find themselves with viable and growing market positions.

Winning the Coming Object War

All this suggests that a rousing object war is on the horizon. Even as they cooperate to set the common standards so necessary to the long-term success of object technology, vendors will be duking it out with each other in the object marketplace, trying to establish solid market positions before the wave passes them by. Anyone following the computer press of late can already see the guns being rolled into position. Vendors are forming alliances left and right around every aspect of object technology. Lines are being drawn and opening salvos fired in such areas as object languages, object databases, object design methodologies and tools, object-oriented graphical user interfaces, and distributed object-management systems.

This all makes good press and is jolly good fun to watch. We can expect hundreds if not thousands of new competing products, a continuous chain of mergers, buyouts, and shifting alliances, and an endless stream of extravagant marketing claims. Throw in a few antitrust suits—or threats of same—and you have an exciting show that looks to be settling in for a long run. But, in reality, which vendor wins the object war is largely irrelevant to computer users, unless they own some stock in one of the major players. That's because the real winner will not be Vendor A or Vendor B, but object technology itself—and, of course, the users who derive the many benefits it has to offer.

No matter what the outcome of the object war, the only sure thing is that, at its end, objects will have become the *lingua franca* of the entire computer software industry. This is no different from saying that the real winner of the PC/mainframe war was not Intel or Apple or Microsoft, but the PC itself—along with the PC user. This may seem like a simple point to make, but it is crucial to anyone seriously considering object technology for their businesses. Those information systems organizations that have survived and prospered throughout the PC wars are not those who backed a specific winning vendor, but rather those that understood that, after it was all over, the desktop and the network—not the mainframe—would call the shots. These organizations developed a successful, vendor-neutral strategy that took the best advantage of the new technology, no matter which vendor was top dog on any given day.

Similarly, should we really care who will be the lucky vendor to ultimately sell us the most objects—the most prevalent object-management environments or the most popular object-development tools? Rest assured, some collection of vendors will fill these needs, whether they are one of the giants of today or merely a gleam in the eye of some precocious teenager. In any case, gone are the days that any one vendor will simply own any area of the computer marketplace. Even mighty Microsoft, which many people feel owns the PC operating system and desktop market, owes its success largely to providing a platform for the software of others.

Microsoft may certainly try to reserve some of the Windows desktop for itself, and it can dictate certain requirements for taking up residence on that desktop. However, the real strength of its desktop strategy is that it basically remains open—available for lease to anyone who cares to move in and follow certain well-known rules. In today's software world, therefore, the concept of private property automatically comes with the clear caveat of equal opportunity housing. So, while some lucky vendors may indeed come to own a piece of the object market, we also know that they can do so only if they follow a set of well-known standards. Whether these standards are laid down explicitly by the OMG or evolve via some other means, the basic result will be the same.

These standards will have to allow all object products to reliably coexist and interoperate with each other, and they will have to support the thousands of object providers and users who will be cropping up in every nook and cranny of the business computing industry. Otherwise, users will quickly reject their offerings in favor of those that do follow such standards. So, from a user's viewpoint, the result is pretty much the same no matter which vendors win the coming object war. They will have to prepare for a future in which reliance on a single vendor or small set of vendors is replaced by an open marketplace of both competing and collaborating objects that all support the same basic interoperability standards.

But, if there's no real reason to care which particular vendors win, then what should business computing users be concerned about in terms of object technology? The answer is really very simple and lies, as the famous saying goes, within ourselves. What these users should be most concerned about is how to best move their own organizations and computing infrastructure to objects. What they really need is a viable strategy that guarantees that, regardless of who comes out on top in the object business, they themselves will derive real business benefits from this important industry transition. In other words, the really interesting question is not so much which computer *vendors* will win the object war, but rather which *users* will survive it and go on to prosper after it's over.

OBJECTS IN YOUR BUSINESS MAY BE CLOSER THAN THEY APPEAR

The rush is already on for businesses to radically restructure themselves—and in a hurry. This movement, generally called *business reengineering*, suggests that businesses continuously reinvent themselves in response to changing business conditions. In short, they do this by constantly reassessing their goals, resources, and strategies, and by developing new ways to recombine and reposition these to gain competitive advantage in an ever-changing marketplace.

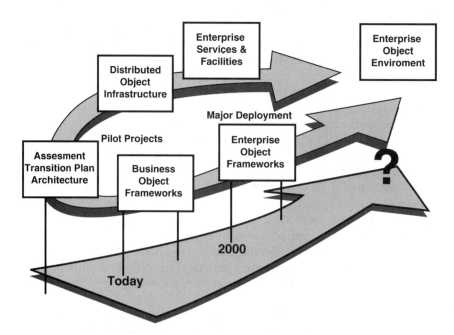

Timeline for Enterprise-wide Object Technology Transition.

For example, let's consider the mythical shoe company, Forever Footwear, that I profiled earlier. Basically a manufacturing company, over the years, Forever began to sell through a widening variety of channels, including mail order, where it enjoyed a good deal of success. At some point, Forever might reassess its marketing strengths and resources, and decide to *reengineer* itself in the direction of the mail-order business, its strongest marketing channel. While still selling shoes and related accessories, it might decide to expand its offering by carrying the footwear lines of other manufacturers, and even to phase out some of its own marginal manufacturing operations in favor of other suppliers.

This is hardly a novel scenario—it literally happens every day. In fact, there is hardly a large or even midsize company with the competitive luxury to *not* go through such self-examination on a regular basis. So, we might ask, what is the process that a company like Forever would go through to reach this conclusion? Well, they would probably start by identifying the key elements of their existing business—customers, products, marketing channels, management and employee skill sets and experience, and so on. They would then describe the behavior of these elements, including their relationship to one another. As this self-examination continued, they might move on to describing the various processes that these elements participate in, including a formal description of the various inputs and outputs each element is responsible for.

Hey, wait a minute. Doesn't this sound a lot like the process of object-oriented analysis and design that I described earlier? That's right, but instead of analyzing computing problems, I'm simply applying the same approach to analyzing ordinary business problems, regardless of whether they have an explicit computing component.

Now, is object technology really as handy for looking at business problems as it is for looking at computing problems? The simple answer is *yes*. There's absolutely no reason to assume that the right place to start with object technology is down in the programming department, or the database department, or even the design department. In fact, maybe the best place to start isn't in the traditional information systems area at all. Maybe the best place to introduce objects is inside the company boardroom, or down the hall in the offices of the CEO and COO.

Objects from the Top Down

Now, suppose the top management of Forever decided to use objects right from the start—build them right into their business reengineering process? Let's say that, in the process of reviewing and reorganizing all the different parts of their business, they described all their new, key business elements and processes as objects, and carefully detailed all the inputs, outputs, and relationships among the various business objects in a coherent schema—what I'll call a *business object model.*

Let's also suppose that the management of Forever sent these results down to its information systems organization and said, "This is our business object model. Please build systems to suit." Right away, Forever's information systems analysts could start examining all the different business objects, analyzing which ones needed what kind of automated support, how these were related to each other, what general functionality they require, and so on. When they were done, these information systems analysts could then formally describe their computing environment in what I'll call a *business object computing model architecture.* This architecture would describe all the business computing objects that are needed at Forever to support all the components of its business object model.

Generating a computing model in this way is truly a novel idea. Most information systems organizations have some kind of architecture on which to base their computing model. However, this architecture is typically organized around the configuration of hardware and systems software that it will support, not on the overall business requirements. In fact, if you ask the average CIO for his or her organization's computing architecture, you'll probably get a complicated picture showing computing platforms, networks, communications lines, and protocols—lots of boxes and arrows with funny names and acronyms attached. Rarely is there anything in this picture that someone on the business side of the house could easily recognize.

And, what if you point to one of the boxes in the picture and ask, "What is this for?" In that case, you're likely to get the answer, "Well, you see, it's really very simple. All our PC users gain access to their host-based applications either through TN3270 or SQL*Net TCP/IP, all of which require this same transport layer provided by NFS. Any other questions?" Now, of course, if your CIO is worth anything at all, that answer is sure to be technically correct. However, it's still pretty useless to the average business person. If the CIO comes by later on and says, "Oh, by the way, I need about another million to upgrade the NFS software we discussed last year," what is the CEO or COO really supposed to say?

But, at Forever, suppose the answer was something like this: "That component of our object computing architecture, called the Customer Object Management Service, handles the transport and mapping of information from a variety of external sources into customer objects for use across the enterprise. These customer-objects are the same ones you defined for us in the business object model you gave us last quarter, and they use exactly the same interfaces. Now that we have a fully implemented version of this service, everyone in the company has access to the same set of customer-objects no matter what platform they are running on."

Give that CIO a raise *and* a promotion! Finally, here is something the Forever CEO and COO—and even many of the end users—can really understand. No more puzzling over a lot of arcane acronyms. Now, if Forever's CIO comes back in a year and says, "I need to spend another million bucks to upgrade the Customer Object Management Service so that it can reliably reach our new field offices in Europe," at least everyone can figure out what business need they're being asked to spend all that money on.

Objects from the Bottom Up

Just having a business object computing architecture, no matter how impressive, doesn't crunch any numbers by itself. Eventually this architecture has to be implemented on something real, something more like a traditional computing architecture, with hardware platforms, systems software, and lots of strange and wonderful acronyms.

So, let's suppose that Forever has finished a first pass at its business object computing architecture, and everyone, including the CEO and COO, feels pretty sure that this architecture meets the computing service requirements of the business object model defined earlier. Now it's time to crank out some real business object services that they can use to build their desired applications. Fortunately for Forever, their omniscient CIO has already begun the process of defining a comprehensive set of lower-level object-systems services that would support the creation, storage, retrieval, distribution, security, and so on of all of their required business computing objects. Using information gleaned from the OMG and other sources, Forever's CIO has been pulling all these together into a coherent *object services model*.

These systems services are, of course, described as a set of objects, with well-known interfaces intended to be accessed by the various business service objects. For example, when any business object needs to store itself, it will know to go to the object storage service and will know how to interface properly to that service. It is hoped that Forever can buy most of the low-level object services straight from its favorite set of vendors, rather than have to invent them itself. And, it is hoped, all these vendor-supplied services will work nicely together, because they follow the same set of interoperability standards.

Assuming this is so, all Forever has to do now is map the processing requirements of its *business computing model* to the interfaces of its *object-systems model*. This should tell it exactly what features of the object-systems model are most important and most heavily used. This is a good way to determine which of the competing object-services products that Forever will be considering from different vendors is best suited to support Forever's enterprise-wide business requirements.

For example, suppose that Forever discovers that most object message traffic can be handled locally in each LAN, with very few messages going between LANs. On the other hand, it may determine that each LAN server will need a lot of object storage to cache customer data coming from an existing mainframe database that will be used to create the very objects that they will be passing around inside the LAN.

This kind of information is crucial to determine what mix of hardware, networks, systems software, and object services is really required to support Forever's business object model. With that kind of information in hand, Forever's analysts can select a company-wide configuration of hardware and software (or integrate it into its existing computing environment) in a way that it can feel confident will handle the load of its enterprise-wide business object model for some time to come.

Objects, Through and Through

With this entire object architecture in place, Forever now has objects from top and bottom. On top is a business object model developed and blessed by the business itself as the fountain of all business knowledge. Below that is a business object computing architecture that describes all the computing services needed to support that business object model. Below the business object computing architecture are the business object services themselves. These take advantage of a robust set of object-system services provided by object vendors, running on an enterprise-wide network of distributed servers, databases, workstations, and legacy systems.

Now Forever can finally start to think about delivering actual applications. Of course, since the business object portion of the architecture is already completely designed and implemented, the applications themselves should be relatively simple to build. In fact, most applications will just be workflow scripts that allow users to access and update the various business objects and services, and move those objects around to other users. Now the various Forever business units can crank out new applications right and left to their heart's content, all based on a set of common business objects.

Furthermore, as the various underlying business objects and business object services are updated by the information-systems organization to reflect changes in the business environment, these user applications will automatically adjust to the new business rules because they operate on top of those business objects and services. Therefore, maintenance will be focused on the common business objects, not the applications themselves.

Similarly, hardware and software products may come and go at the lower levels of the architecture, as long as the new products still provide the same basic object services and interfaces to the business object services above them. This way, the information systems group can upgrade to new hardware, change vendors, or create new services, all without disrupting any currently running applications. Is this a pipe dream, or an opportunity? No doubt about it—if things really could be made to work this way, it would forever change the dynamic of how information systems were defined, created, and maintained.

Today we tend to focus on applications on the one hand and platforms on the other. With objects, however, applications become relatively trivial extensions of the business object services, while platforms are effectively hidden under a layer of platform-neutral systems object services. This suggests that the emerging market for business computing will begin to shift away from both applications and platforms, and toward a kind of business middleware based on both business and systems objects, from which individual businesses will tailor their own unique configurations based on their own unique requirements.

Down at the systems object level, such things as ORBs and Object Services will hold sway. Much like the operating systems of today, this stuff will come bundled with hardware and systems software—commodity items supplied by vendors. Just like business applications today are built to plug into today's operating systems, in tomorrow's computing environment, business objects and objects services will plug into these ORBs and Object Services. There will undoubtedly be a few big winners in the ORB world, just like Microsoft has grabbed a big chunk of the desktop market and Novell a big chunk of the network world. However, the majority of tomorrow's players will be in a different game altogether—either offering tools and services to create and manage business objects, or selling the objects themselves.

This market is just emerging, and it will be some time before most businesses will be able to buy robust generic business objects and object services direct from major vendors. However, in the long run, this is the real growth area for the object business—and the area where the businesses themselves will get the most benefit from vendors. No longer will end users be creating applications from scratch or buying inflexible, off-the-shelf applications and fitting their business around them. Instead, they'll be buying business objects and services from third-party business software specialists and integrating these into their own business object computing model.

As I have said, this won't be happening tomorrow, so those companies making big commitments to objects right now will probably have to homegrow at least a first pass at their business object infrastructure. As you shall see, however, that is not necessarily a bad thing, since it will give those organizations a leg up on their competition in understanding how such business objects will work in their own computing environment once they become mainstream commodities.

GETTING READY FOR OBJECTS

Well, here we are in the last chapter and I still haven't told you exactly what you should be doing about objects yourself. Of course, if this book has been any help at all, you are already doing a lot of thinking about that. And, as Thomas Watson, the founder of IBM, knew so well, that's the first and most important step to understanding what you have to do next. Watson was so enamored with the importance of thinking that he actually had the word *Think* plastered on posters and other paraphernalia all over IBM. The object (no pun intended) of all this was to remind his employees—and even himself—that it was not enough to just continue doing things the old, comfortable way. To truly get ahead, Watson believed, you had to think and rethink everything you did, trying to make it better each time you did it.

Corny as this may sound, there's a lot of truth to it—and it certainly seemed to work well for a long time for Watson and IBM. In our case, I imagine a new version of this slogan—something like *Think Objects*—as a way to remind everyone to rethink what they are doing today in terms of a new, object-oriented approach. Of course, I don't advocate actually plastering placards that say *Think Objects* all over your office—that's too corny even for a pure futurist. But I certainly can imagine trying out a number of different ways to get yourself and the people around you to break out of some of your old ways of dealing with business information problems and learn some new, object-oriented thinking to take their place.

So, the very first thing you can do to prepare yourself for the brave new world of objects is to convince yourself and your colleagues that objects are really a fundamentally different way of viewing the business and business-information systems. If yours is typical, that's not going to be as easy as it sounds. Even armed with the ideas in this book, it is tempting for most information systems professionals to look at objects as just another technology. After all, there's already been structured programming, distributed databases, AI, GUI, CASE, client/server, integrated office, workgroup, EIS, and 100 other industry technology buzzwords, all of which have had their day, and none of which has truly revolutionized our thinking about information systems. Why should objects be different? But object technology *is* different, because it is the first new technology to systematically attack the entire business information system from end to end using the *same* paradigm.

Starting at the very top—the analysis of the business and its critical components—object technology applies the same principles all the way down to the bottom: capturing user input on-screen, sending messages across a network, storing and retrieving complex forms of information, and so on. Even the work of managing the objects is done by *other* objects. This means that, for every way of doing things in the traditional world, there is another, probably better, way of doing the same thing in the object world. You have a heck of a lot of rethinking to do before you and your colleagues *really* have this object thing down pat.

Please believe me—it's not just a question of reading a few books about objects, or writing a few sample programs in C++; I've learned that the hard way. Even after years of experience, there are still things about objects—important things—that I don't yet understand very well. If you are just getting started in objects, I assure you that you have a long way to go.

The Sticky Problem of GUIs

To give you an example of what I mean, just consider one area related to objects that you probably think you already understand—user interfaces. Now, if you grew up in the mainframe world, you no doubt had some utility, such as CICS, that enabled you to draw a screen and, at a certain point in your program, present the screen to the user. The user fills the screen with information and then hits a certain key. The information on the screen fills a buffer and is dumped back into your program, which has been sitting there all along, quietly waiting for the user to finish.

Now, this is fine, as long as you think of the user as someone filling in one screen after another, like a data entry operator typing in a form. In this case, the *program* defines the job, and the *person* is just a slave to the machine. Of course, not only is this fundamentally boring, but, more important, it also has little to do with the way most business professionals work. That's at least one good reason why these systems never caught on with knowledge workers. Anyone who has seen an Apple Macintosh or a PC with Windows already knows that there is a much better way to interface with intelligent, take-charge users. First of all, a user can have as many screens (windows) as he or she chooses at any time. A user can jump around from window to window at will, even copying information from one window and placing it into another. Users can even make changes in one window that automatically change the contents or activity in another window.

Most important, you can show anything you want in a window: text, maps, charts, even 3-D, full-motion video! Meanwhile, the computer can also be calculating your weekly schedule, retrieving data from a host database, receiving electronic mail, and so on, displaying the results in yet other windows or in little animated icons. And, if you hold your mouse pointer over any window, button, or icon, the system cheerfully displays *Help* text that explains what that particular GUI component is all about.

You may already know that all of this nifty stuff is based on objects. Under the covers, all GUIs are object-based: They accept the user input as it happens, and convert these user input events to object-style messages on the various GUI components. When a component receives this kind of message, it simply forwards it to a piece of code (a method) that deals with that kind of message. That's why anyone writing a Windows or Macintosh program might as well program using objects, because they get pretty much the same thing, anyway. However, the real issue I'm trying to get at here is not how GUIs relate to objects—the real issue is objects. Even in just this one area, user interfaces have already fundamentally changed the way we think about computing. Now that we have the kind of GUIs that object technology can give us, it's a bit difficult to settle for the kind of user interface provided by CICS and its imitators.

Now, of course, you can still build a window that looks and acts like a CICS screen, and many people are doing just that. However, the only good reason to do this kind of thing is to make a legacy CICS application available on a PC, not to create new applications. Anyone taking the time and energy to create important new business applications would be out of his or her mind to limit user-interface thinking to what CICS provides. This would be tantamount to planning a new international business venture without considering using the airplane or telephone! But, once we open up the screen to sophisticated GUIs, we have a number of new problems to solve. First, we have the relatively mundane but important problem of training our developers in a whole new way of working, not to mention a different tools set. We also may encounter some problems training the ultimate users; they need to learn how to move around the new interface: use the mouse, move from application to application, and so on.

However, the really big problem is figuring out what to do with all the powerful, new options that a sophisticated GUI can give us. How do we restructure our existing and planned applications to take advantage of the new GUI? What changes can we make to the users' workflow and work habits that will encourage better use of the GUI? And what new classes of applications that we've never tackled before (or tried to tackle before and failed) are now made possible by this new GUI technology?

And what about practical organizational questions: How much is this going to cost? How long will it take? What new tools and platforms do I need? Can my current people make the transition? How do I find the new resources I'll need? What changes to our organizational structure would help? And the toughest of questions: How do I know if I'm really making progress and not just kidding myself?

As you can easily imagine, each of us could spend a lot of time productively thinking, reading, and talking about a subject like GUIs before we ever wrote any significant applications using a GUI tool or platform. There are literally dozens of business and organizational issues that you need to address that are critical to incorporating GUIs into your existing framework that have nothing whatsoever to do with the technical issues of writing GUI code. In fact, smart people started looking at GUIs five or even ten years ago, before there were even decent development or deployment environments for GUI applications. Sure, those people had to work a lot harder to get out their first GUI applications than you have to today, but they also have had five years or more to think about all the other GUI issues that have little or nothing to do with cranking out GUI code.

Now that GUIs are going mainstream, they are well positioned to take full business advantage of all the latest developments. Meanwhile, for their less savvy competitors, GUIs will remain a sticky problem for some time to come. While these laggards are still trying to figure out what to make of GUIs, their more aggressive competitors will already be reaping the benefits of being able to provide a whole new generation of important, GUI-based applications to their business users. But, if this is true for GUIs alone, just think about what that must mean for objects in general. GUIs are just one little corner of object technology. There are lots bigger nuts to crack in such areas as distributed object management, object architecture and design, business object frameworks and services, and all the other things I've talked about at length in this book. If even one-tenth of what I have discussed becomes *real* in the next ten years, that alone would be enough to keep every CIO in the world up a lot later at night than usual.

So much for any temptation to do little or nothing until the object cows come home. Any information systems professional who is just sitting around waiting for objects to happen is likely to have a rude surprise when objects finally do settle in. At that point, there will be more than enough business competitors who have already taken the plunge into objects and are just itching to march into battle against those still holdingoutontheMaginotlineoftraditionalinformation-systemsthinking.

Object Show and Tell

Instead of waiting around, one very important thing you should do is to begin actively collecting all the information you can find on object technology. A great way to do this is to attend important, object-industry trade shows. Once you're inside, you can collect written information and pick the brains of exhibitors and presenters alike.

The object industry is still very young and fast-moving, and is likely to remain so for quite a while. Trade shows, such as the OMG's Object World, are excellent sources of information on current thinking and practice. Lots of new ideas are percolating at the better shows, both in terms of products being displayed by vendors and seminars being given by industry luminaries. So much new stuff is going on that even an old hand like me can find lots of interesting things to see and do. For new initiates, however, these shows can be big eye-openers. Most newcomers are amazed to find out how much work is being done with objects in so many areas. In many cases, they talk to experts who have direct experience doing object development in their specific line of business. Unfortunately, many organizations don't always take the best advantage of these shows, losing a valuable source of information. Many think that object technology is just for developers, so they send only their programmers and designers, and not their project managers, planning personnel, or business managers. Others skip these shows altogether on the mistaken premise that the shows will make sense only if they are currently working on an object project.

Of course, trade shows are not the only sources of information on objects. There are such books as this one, as well as a number of trade magazines and scholarly journals. These are important and inexpensive sources of information that can give you a reasonably good idea of the scope of object technology above and beyond simple programming and design issues. You can update and refine this information through direct contact with experts available at many good trade shows.

Another source of information is available from industry organizations interested in objects: ACM's OOPSLA and the OMG are both good examples. These organizations regularly publish lots of documents examining the finer points of object technology in depth. In the case of the OMG, many of these documents describe current or projected object standards that you'd better know about, anyway.

Verily I Say, Assess Thyself

Once you are comfortable speaking object-lingo, one of the very next things that you can do is to undertake a self-directed object assessment of your own company. During this self-assessment, you should look at your current organization; inventory its skills, experiences, and structure; and determine what, if anything, might have to change before you can really move forward in object technology. This kind of self-assessment is good even if you already have some object-technology projects under way. You may already have some hotshot object developers on staff, and they may be great C++ or Smalltalk programmers but they won't necessarily be able to identify any organizational problems that could impede your progress.

In fact, this kind of assessment should be directed by someone with some serious experience in object technology, and preferably someone who has done these assessments before for other large organizations. If no one currently in your organization comes to mind, recruit this kind of person or hire a consultant, because you'll find that you definitely need their expertise over time. This kind of self-assessment typically begins with an inventory of skills and experience within your organization relevant to object technology. As suggested earlier, there may already be some object-oriented projects under way; if so, you might want an honest and knowledgeable opinion from someone other than the participants as to how far along these really are. Besides any such projects, some of the staff may have received some experience or training in objects before they came to work at your company. Sometimes this is overlooked—a mistake, given the fact that internal experience is often the cheapest and best experience you can get your hands on.

Another big area of assessment is how clearly the various parts of your business and information systems organization see the need for objects, and their view of the relationship between object technology and the main business objectives of the enterprise. Some people who are critical to the success of any new initiative may have radically different or deeply interesting views about these subjects that everyone should be aware of as soon as possible.

There are lots more important assessment areas I could describe at length, but this is not the appropriate forum. Suffice it to say here that doing this kind of assessment up front and discussing it in full with everyone who should be interested is a healthy exercise that will both elevate the discussion of object technology with the organization and provide a zero milepost for measuring how object technology will be affecting that organization in the future.

Laying a Solid Foundation

Once an organization has learned enough about objects and itself to begin some serious work, it is time to lay a solid foundation for future work in object technology by creating a comprehensive transition plan and by simultaneously developing a comprehensive object architecture. Even more than the assessment, both of these efforts is far more sizable and detailed than I can explain here. In fact, either one of them could easily fill a book all by itself. However, I feel that they are both so important to the future success of any major object venture that I must give each of them at least a cursory overview here.

A transition plan is basically designed to take your organization from where it is today (as determined in the assessment) to some point in the future when objects will be a significant part of your computing environment. The transition plan is not just a project plan for one or a few pilot object projects, although it certainly may include such projects. Instead, think of the transition plan as a road map for all future work in object technology, and as far ahead as possibe. A truly comprehensive transition plan deals in a large number of areas, including project selection, training, staff augmentation and organization, tools selection and integration, platform migration, performance metrics, and so on. In each of these areas, the transition plan will explain how the organization will incorporate object technology into its traditional structures and processes, and/or modify those structures and processes as needed.

Without such a transition plan, learning about and using object technology can take place only in an ad hoc manner. Unfortunately, organizations can stumble along for years without developing such a plan in the mistaken feeling that they are still making incremental progress. In most such cases, however, they are really making considerably less progress than they could in most areas, and completely spinning their wheels in others. Without a plan, however, it is not only impossible to correct this, but it is also often difficult for the organization itself to figure out what is happening—until something drastic must be done.

What I have just described could apply equally to making a transition to any new technology (e.g., client/server, GUI, databases, etc.) without a good plan. However, the problems associated with not having such a plan are magnified when it comes to object technology, since, as discussed before, it is likely to affect so many areas of business and the information system organization. As a result, the transition planning effort needs to be led by at least one person who has gone through a similar transition before. However, just having an experienced person is not enough. For the transition plan to be successful, it must engage the active attention of every key manager in both the business and information systems organizations most likely to be affected by the move to object technology.

One key element of the plan is a major effort in its own right—developing an object architecture. I discussed this architecture briefly above, describing how a business would build both a business object model and computing object model and then tie them together into a comprehensive, end-to-end object model. A good first pass at such an object architecture clearly needs to be done before planning, much less implementing, any serious object applications, making any major platform selection or configuration decisions, or attempting to integrate or migrate any important legacy applications. Obviously, until some basic object architecture is in place, the transition plan can deal with only very preliminary and peripheral transition issues.

Developing a good object architecture requires a team of people to make a close review of the business objects and current computing environment, and analyze and reorganize them into a comprehensive object model. And, like the assessment and the transition plan, an object architecture effort needs to be led by at least one person already experienced in developing such architectures. The output of the object architecture effort is not only a written, formal object model, but is also a consensus among the architecture team in terms of definitions, concepts, analytical approach, and process. As future work proceeds, the architecture will remain an important touchstone to which the various project management and development teams can compare their work and through which they can integrate their results.

If this preceding discussion about transition planning and architecture sounded a bit heavier in tone that the rest of this book, that's because they are definitely ten-ton subjects that are hard to make amusing or engaging. They remain the first major challenge of any organization trying to get into objects in any serious and lasting way, and deserve far more weight and volume than I can afford to give them here.

We've Only Just Begun

The really good news is that there is still plenty of time for prospective users of object technology to get on the stick and develop realistic plans that will keep them in step, or even a little ahead, of their competition in this area. Only a few organizations have already progressed so far into object technology that they are clearly ahead of the pack in their respective industries. Therefore, this is a really good time for you and your organization to take a new and hard look at your own view of object technology. Do you still think, even after reading this book, that it's probably a fad? Do you think it's a great idea but one whose time is still too far off to be useful? Do you think it's the thing to do, but despair the thought of ever getting your own hidebound business to adopt it?

All these are very common and reasonable ways to feel at this point in the life span of the object industry. I hope that I have dispelled at least some of the myths or simple misunderstandings about object technology that hold people back from exploring it further. However, I won't be particularly surprised if you still have some doubts and fears. It usually takes more than a book or two to move people along. I'll be glad if you have moved a step or two farther down your own personal object road because of what I have said in these pages.

Glossary

This glossary contains definitions of the technical abbreviations and terms used throughout this book. The acronyms common to the object industry are listed first, followed by an alphabetized list of technical terms and definitions.

ACM—Association of Computing Machinery. A public organization specifically devoted to informing its members about object technology.

AI—See *Artificial Intelligence.*

ANSI—American National Standards Institute

BOD—The OMG's Board of Directors

CASE tools—Computer Aided Software Engineering tools.

COBOL—One of many high-level business computing languages that enable programmers to write human-readable source code that can be automatically converted into computer-readable programs by compilers.

CORBA—Common ORB Architecture

COSS—Common OS Standard

DOS—See *Disk Operating System.*

GUI—See *Graphical User Interface.*

IDL—Interface Definition Language. A vital part of the CORBA standard that looks like the part of C++ that defines classes, with extensions to handle distributed messaging. Programmers implement their objects in any language they like, then describe the interface for each class of object in IDL.

IT—See *Information Technology.*

LAN—Local Area Network. (See *Network.*)

MIP—See *Millions of Instructions per Second.*

ODBMG—Object Database Management Group

OLE—Microsoft's *Object Linking and Embedding* specification

OLTP—On Line Transactional Processing

OMA—Object Management Architecture

OMG—The Object Management Group

OOPSLA—Object-Oriented Programming, Languages, Systems, and Applications

ORB—See *Object Request Broker.*

OSF—The Open Software Foundation

OSTF—The Object Services Task Force

PCTE—Portable Common Tools Environment

RFP—Request For Proposals

SIG—Special Interest Group. A group of users on a network or electronic bulletin board who form a group to discuss a common interest via e-mail.

TC—The OMG's Technical Committee

TF—Task Force

Application—A software package that accomplishes a specific, predefined set of related tasks.

Architecture—The high-level software design that application developers use as a blueprint for their work.

Artificial Intelligence (AI)—Software that attempts to mimic the subtle machinations of human intelligence. AI relies on oddly named abstractions, such as *neural networks, fuzzy logic,* and *game theory,* to model human intuition and creativity.

Behavior—The various things that real-world entities are capable of doing. Objects mimic real-world behavior through a set of software subroutines called methods. (See also: *Object, Method.*)

Brute-Force Argument—Any argument based on the premise that bigger and more powerful is always better. Often applied to hardware designs or software solutions that stress raw power over elegance and appropriateness.

Business Reengineering—The continuous self-reinvention that businesses undertake in response to ever-changing business conditions.

C++—A set of object-oriented extensions added to a nonobject-oriented, high-level software programming language called C.

Centralized Control—A once-popular business strategy that carried corporate self-sufficiency to remarkable extremes. Adherents attempted to provide the vast majority of their own support functions in an effort to maintain control over quality, price, customers, intellectual property, and every other aspect of their business.

Class—A useful grouping of objects that is based on the behavior and state that they have in common. (See also: *Behavior, Object, State.*)

Class Dependency—A potentially negative side effect associated with object classes: Changes in one object class, if not properly managed, can trigger cascading waves of change that effect *dependent* classes in ways not easily predicted.

Class Library—A software repository that contains a blueprint for each object class in the system. The class blueprints are used each time a new instance of a class is constructed. (See also: *Class, Instance, Object.*)

Class Repository—Any facility that keeps an inventory of previously developed object-classes in a convenient classification system that enables intelligent retrieval. A class repository can be anything from a developer's brain, to a chart on the wall, to a company-wide database, to a worldwide automated database specifically designed to handle object-class definitions.

Client—A software entity that uses the software services provided by software *servers*. (See also: *Client-Server Model, Server.*)

Client-Server Model—One of many abstract models used by software designers. In the Client-Server model, *client* software entities use software services provided by software *server* entities. (See also: *Client, Server.*)

Common Object Model—An *object model* (a precise description of what it means to be an object in a given system) that most object systems adhere to. A common object model specifies the terminology used to describe and specify objects, the manner in which an object communicates with other objects, and the relationships an object can have with other objects.

Compiler—A software program that converts the human-readable *source* code that programmers create into computer readable *object* code that can be linked to *libraries* of subroutines to create a single binary file that computers can run as a program.

Context—The specific *point of view* of a given object or other software entity.

Data Structure—A set of closely related informational elements stored together so that they can be loaded in computer memory and efficiently accessed as needed.

De Facto Standards—Unofficial suggested standards that are standards *in fact*, if not in the eyes of official standards groups. (See also: *De Jure Standards, Standards.*)

De Jure Standards—Official standards promulgated by a recognized standards organization capable of revising and enforcing the standards they set. (See also: *De Facto Standards, Standards.*)

Disk Operating System (DOS)—An operating system for PCs that was named after IBM's mainframe DOS.

Distributed Software—Modularized software applications whose modules can be split apart and stored on different computers within the same network. (See also: *Application, Network.*)

Downsizing—A business strategy in which corporations reassess their business goals and practices in hopes of reducing bureaucracy while decentralizing corporate control.

Dynamic Invocation—A CORBA mechanism that enables clients to construct requests *on the fly* without going through stubs. (See also: *Client, CORBA, Stubs.*)

Electronic Mail (abbreviated as e-mail)—Mail designed to be sent electronically over computer networks.

Encapsulation—The containment of *state* information and behavioral *methods* within a software entity called an object. (See also: *Method, Object, State.*)

Fault Tolerance—The capability designed into software applications that enables them to continue functioning after encountering a fault or error.

Federated Addressing—An addressing scheme that enables any object in a system to send a request-message to any object in any other collaborating object system, all without knowing anything about the precise location of that object or its object system. (See also: *Federation, Object, Request.*)

Federation—A message-passing system based upon an addressing scheme in which messages are forwarded by a series of intermediaries without the need for a central repository that knows every address. The intermediaries need not know anything about the sender or recipient of the message (or even about the other intermediaries in the delivery chain or the content of the message) to deliver each message quickly and accurately. Examples include post offices and phone companies. (See also: *Federated Addressing, Object, Request*.)

Graphical User Interface (GUI)—The graphics on a computer's screen that computer users interact with to run their computers. Today's Graphical User Interfaces for PCs and workstations enable users to manipulate intuitive, user-friendly devices (e.g., a mouse or a joystick) to interact with *icons, windows*, and other dynamic on-screen GUI graphics. (See also: *Icon, Window*.)

Heterogeneous—An adjective that describes a computer network containing computers of more than one design or more than one manufacturer.

Homogeneous—An adjective that describes a computer network in which all computers are of the same general type or are from the same manufacturer.

Icon—A small, on-screen graphic symbol that users manipulate to control the icon's underlying software application.

Implementation—The specific software code that is used to implement a general architectural design.

Information Technology (IT)—Hardware and software technology that enables businesses to store and retrieve large amounts of electronic information.

Infrastructure—The combination of software services and other related resources that provides the foundation for a complete software environment.

Instance—A specific object constructed from an object-class blueprint. Each instance is given a unique identifier code to differentiate it from all other objects in the system.

Instance Management—The software mechanism that comes into play every time any object is created, activated, shared, changed, destroyed, moved, stored, retrieved, secured, accessed, or otherwise operated upon.

Interface—The names and data requirements of all the public methods in a given object. (See also: *Method, Object*.)

Interoperability—The degree to which object classes are capable of exchanging information and requests within the same system. Also, the degree to which different but complementary applications are capable of accessing each other's information and functionality.

Language Mapping—A concept that allows clients to make requests through the syntax of their own programming language without being directly aware of either stubs or dynamic invocation. (See also: *Client, CORBA, Stubs*.)

Local Area Network (LAN)—A network made up of computers in relatively close physical proximity.

Macro Languages—Simplified programming languages that can be mastered by nonprogrammers. Often designed for use with electronic spreadsheets and word-processor software.

Mainframe—An expensive monolithic computer whose primary advantages are high processing speed and large storage capacity. Disadvantages include high initial cost, expensive proprietary software, and high maintenance requirements.

Meganet—An imaginary global supernetwork introduced in this book as an exercise in futuristic thinking.

Method—A set of software modules stored inside an object that, when invoked, produces the behavior associated with the object.

Microprocessor—A chip that acts as the heart of a computer, routing data throughout the computer system the same way that a heart routes blood through a living organism.

Millions of Instructions per Second—A measurement benchmark of raw computing speed.

Multitasking—A trait of many modern operating systems that enables them to run multiple programs simultaneously, automatically switching from program to program as required.

Network—A loosely coupled group of computers that communicate through high speed, high bandwidth. Networks are described as *homogeneous* if their computers are all of the same general type (or are all from the same manufacturer) and *heterogeneous* if they contain computers of more than one design or more than one manufacturer. (See also: *Heterogeneous, Homogeneous*.)

Node—An individual computer in a network.

Object—A reusable, self-contained software component that holds (encapsulates) information about its own *state* and behavioral software modules called *methods*. (See also: *Encapsulation, Method, State.*)

Object Database—A long-term repository where objects *persist* (hang around) during the times that they are not actively residing in short-term computer memory.

Object Interface—The names and data requirements of all the public methods in a given object. (See also: *Method, Object.*)

Objective C—A set of object-oriented extensions added to a non-object-oriented high-level software programming language called C.

Object Management—The set of issues and problems related to managing objects in large-scale systems. Object management is a separate subject from object architecture, which deals with how *individual* applications or closely related sets of applications are best carved up into useful objects and classes.

Object Management Group (OMG)—By far the largest and most broadly based organization devoted exclusively to object technology. The OMG promotes object standards and guides the development and commercialization of object technologies. Its range of standards activities are the most comprehensive, and its decisions are the most widely accepted by vendors and users alike.

Object Relationships—Software objects, like the real-world business entities they model, maintain several different kinds of relationships with other objects. These relationships range from simple communicational relationships, in which objects make requests of other objects, to complex, rules-based relationships.

Object Request Broker—A specialized object that expedites the exchange of requests among other objects in an object-oriented software environment.

Object Revolution—The worldwide paradigm shift that is already taking place from traditional software design to object-oriented design.

Object Service—Short for Object Management Service. Every time one object instance makes a request of another, the receiving object is providing an *object service* for the sending object. Object management services work with objects of all (or at least a broad range of) classes. They allow programmers to manipulate objects that are largely independent of the behavior they derive from their classes. (See also: *Request, Server.*)

Object World—The OMG's annual trade show, the largest trade show devoted to commercial object technology. Run in partnership with IDG

World Expo, a large computer trade show producer. Started as an annual event in San Francisco in the summer of 1991, it has grown to include annual satellite shows in Boston, London, Tokyo, Sydney, and Frankfurt.

Open Systems—Nonproprietary hardware or software systems that adhere to standards designed to encourage use by others.

Operating System—Software that insulates programmers and users from changes in the hardware configuration by keeping track of software files and managing other important computing resources, such as disk drives, printers, and memory.

Paradigm—An abstract model on which designers base real-world computer software designs.

Parallel Processing—Short for parallel data processing. A faster, more efficient alternative to serial processing (the traditional form of processing, in which data flows through a microprocessor in a single stream controlled by one software process at a time). Parallel processing divides the data stream into several small, independently controlled *threads* that pass simultaneously through as many processing chips as the computer system can provide.

Persistence Services—Services that enable objects to *persist* (hang around) during the times that they are not actively residing in RAM. The terms *object persistence system* and *object database* currently mean the same thing.

Power User—A technically savvy user who knows enough to write or customize software applications.

Request—A message sent from one object to another that usually contains three things: an ID number that identifies the object that is the recipient of the request, a method from the object's interface, and an exact value for each piece of required information. (See also: *Interface, Method, Object.*)

Rightsizing—See *Downsizing*.

Server—A software entity that provides software services to multiple software *clients*. (See also: *Client, Client-Server Model.*)

Silicon Valley—Originally, a valley in Northern California that attracted an unusually large number of computer-related startup companies and high-technology businesses. More recently, a similar high-tech area anywhere in the world.

Skeletons—Software entities generated by an IDL compiler. Skeletons are the mechanism that the ORB uses to call objects. (See also: *Object, ORB, Stubs.*)

Skunk Works—A corporate research facility physically separated from the parent company and operated like an independent startup group. One of the earliest and most famous skunk works was at Xerox's Palo Alto Research Center (PARC).

Smalltalk—The first language in which absolutely everything is treated as an object. Most common notions of objects today—classes, requests, instances—were first implemented in Smalltalk.

Software—The brains of the computer. Software determines not only how the computer interacts with users and other computers, but also how the computer uses its peripherals.

Specifications—Exact technical descriptions of the architectural design, range of functionality, and interactive nature (often called *look and feel*) of a single software package or integrated group of packages. (See also: *Standards*.)

Standards—Software specifications that have been officially promulgated by recognized standards organizations that have been granted the legal authority to enforce the standards they disseminate. (See also: *Specifications*.)

State—Information that is encapsulated in objects in the form of variables. Each state variable is given a name that indicates its contents, but the contents themselves cannot be accessed except by companion software modules called *methods*. Encapsulation ensures that state information inside an object doesn't get fouled up accidentally. (See also: *Encapsulation, Method, Object*.)

Stubs—Software entities generated by an IDL compiler. Stubs are the mechanisms that clients use to actually call the ORB with their requests. (See also: *Object, ORB, Skeletons*.)

Virtual Corporation—A business entity with a very flat management hierarchy and well-focused skills set that makes its money through strategic alliances arranged among semiautonomous units of the corporation, or between those units and various outside businesses.

Virtual Machine—A theoretical computing environment for individual software applications that always appears to be as big as it needs to be, no matter how much hardware is actually available at any given time.

Virtual Mininets—Small virtual computer networks that unite all or part of a business computing system for the required processing of its joint operations. (See also: *Virtual Machine*.)

Whetstone Test—Benchmarking software that rates computing speed.

White Room—A secure centralized data processing room in a traditional corporation or similar entity. Derives its name from its brilliantly lit, operating-theater-like atmosphere.

Window—A movable, resizable, rectangular space on a computer's screen, in which a single application's GUI appears while the application is running.

Workgroup—A group of employees whose work assignments require them to share business-related resources over the same computer networks. Employees in a workgroup environment often work in separate physical environments. (See also: *Network*.)

Workstation—A powerful computer designed for professionals who require more computing power than can be squeezed out of the average, garden-variety PC.

Index